# AMERICAN CATHOLICISM

## Where Do We Go from Here?

George Devine

*Seton Hall University*

PRENTICE-HALL, INC.                    *Englewood Cliffs, N.J.*

*Library of Congress Cataloging in Publication Data*

DEVINE, GEORGE, 1941–
  American Catholicism: where do we go from here?

  1. Catholic Church in the United States.
2. Catholic Church—Doctrinal and controversial works—
Catholic authors. I. Title.
BX1406.2.D45       230'.2        74-11182
ISBN 0-13-203986-0
ISBN 0-13-023978-X (pbk.)

10 9 8 7 6 5 4 3 2 1

PRENTICE-HALL INTERNATIONAL, INC., London
PRENTICE-HALL OF AUSTRALIA, PTY. LTD., Sydney
PRENTICE-HALL OF CANADA, LTD., Toronto
PRENTICE-HALL OF INDIA PRIVATE LIMITED, New Delhi
PRENTICE-HALL OF JAPAN, INC., Tokyo

**Acknowledgments**

I would like to express my appreciation for use of the following:

Excerpt from *The New York Times* of February 4, 1973, © 1973 by The New York Times Company. Reprinted by permission.

Excerpts from "The Last of the American Irish Fade Away" by Andrew M. Greeley, © 1971 by The New York Times Company. Reprinted by permission.

Excerpts from *The Sandbox Tree* by Thomas Fleming, © 1970 by William Morrow & Co., Inc. Reprinted by permission.

Excerpts from *The National Catholic Reporter*. Reprinted by permission.

Excerpts from the sermon by Rev. Dr. Paul A. Crow, Jr. Reprinted by permission of the Consultation on Church Union.

Excerpts from "Catholicism Midwest Style" in *America* and *The Documents of Vatican II*. Reprinted with permission from *America*, © 1966. All Rights Reserved. America Press, Inc., New York, N.Y. 10019.

Excerpts reprinted from *Overview*. Published by the Thomas More Association, 180 N. Wabash Ave., Chicago, Ill. 60601. Reprinted by permission.

Excerpts from *Christ Acts Through Sacraments* by A.-M. Roguet. Published by the Liturgical Press. Copyrighted by the Order of St. Benedict, Inc., Collegeville, Minnesota. Reprinted by permission.

Excerpts from *Transformation in Christ* by George Devine, © 1972 by the Pious Society of St. Paul, Inc. Reprinted by permission from Alba House.

Excerpt from *Living Worship* as reprinted in *Overview*, © 1973 by *Living Worship*, a publication of The Liturgical Conference. Reprinted by permission.

For my brother

# Contents

Foreword                                                    *vii*

Abbreviations                                                  *x*

1    In the World, But Not Of It?                              *1*

     *Catholic views of the Church and its members vis-à-vis
     the* saeculum *amid the changes of the late twentieth
     century in the wake of Vatican Council II  •  The
     "secular city" and the new theological views of think-
     ers like Teilhard deChardin, Rahner, and Schille-
     beeckx*

2    A Holy Nation, A Royal Priesthood                        *20*

     *The traditional role of the Catholic priest and of
     religious-order members in the Catholic community
     •  New crises and opportunities for clerical, lay, and
     religious-order leadership in the American Church*

*v*

**3**    **Teach Us How to Pray**    *43*

*Changes in the Mass and other liturgical rites since Vatican Council II • Crises in Catholic belief and piety in the 1960s and early 1970s • New roles of liturgy and prayer in Catholic life in America*


**4**    **The One True Church?**    *60*

*Changes in Catholics' ways of relating to other religions intellectually and theologically, as well as personally and socially • The impact of the ecumenical movement and its current problems*


**5**    **A "New Morality" for Catholics?**    *77*

*Traditional Catholic understandings of magisterial authority, morality based on natural law, and the teaching of the Church • Crises in contemporary morality for American Catholics (Vietnam, contraception, etc.) and how these are being dealt with and understood by the Catholics of America*


**6**    **Where Do We Go from Here?**    *94*

*Possible future trends in the American Catholic experience*

# Foreword

Every author tries to start off by telling his readers just what his book will be about. I should like to do the same, but also to make clear what this book will *not* be about.

On the one hand, this is a book in religious studies, in that it attempts some investigation of Roman Catholicism on the modern American scene. It is not, however, a theological book in the strict sense of that term. Rather, it will attempt to describe American Catholicism from a variety of angles, one of which will surely be theological.

This book will not attempt in any way a detailed history of Catholicism or of Catholics in America, which a number of other authors have done, some quite recently and some quite well. However, it should be recognized at once that any understanding of Catholicism in any context —particularly within the context of America in the middle of the twentieth century and in all probability for the remainder of this century—will necessarily incorporate a certain understanding of and empathy for the Catholic past. This point is especially important when it is remembered that Catholics the world over, and Catholics in America in particular, are just now beginning to come to terms with what has been a most complex and confusing series of changes in even the smallest details—*especially* the smallest details—of a routine which for so many came to be identified with the Church and its tenets. To understand where American Catholics and American Catholicism are today, and where they might be going in the near future, we must see where they were on the eve of this era of turbulent and bewildering change.

It will be evident that the changes which have affected American Catholics have by no means been limited to religious or ecclesiastical spheres. Rather, these have taken place in the context of the political, social, economic, cultural and ultimately personal changes which Americans in general and Catholics in particular remember as characteristic of the middle and late 1960s. We are all well aware that for some the changes were too fast and furious, just as for others they were too few and far between, and for others yet too little and too late. In any case, American Catholics and American Catholicism will tend to be measuring their self-images against the background of these changes and the implications attached thereto.

The responses of American Catholics individually, or of the Catholic Church in the United States, to various questions occasioned by change will be far from univocal. Two decades ago, one could think with some facility in terms of a "Catholic position" on just about every conceivable subject. Those days are gone, and I think they are gone forever. Some are sorry to see them gone, since this departure seems also to mean the departure of easy certainty; some of these will even attempt to restore that atmosphere of certainty, even by means which the objective observer would immediately identify as patently artificial. But gone they are, and for American Catholics the questions "Who are we?" and "Where do we go from here?" are important, perplexing, and sometimes laden with emotion and even trepidation.

This volume will hardly attempt definitive answers to such questions. What I will attempt to do is outline some chief areas of Catholic concern, especially in this country, before, during and in the wake of the events of the middle and late 1960s, and as these appear to be shaping up for at least the immediately foreseeable future—possibly, even for the remainder of the twentieth century. On the basis of my own experience and investigations, and with gratitude to those who have shared with me their own experiences and investigations, I will endeavor to describe (although hardly *define!*)—for the student of religion in America and for the general reader as well—what it has meant and what it might mean to be Catholic in America.

All those who have participated in or articulated the American Catholic experience have been in part authors of this work. It has been my own task to reflect and comment on that experience and what it might mean for the future of America and the future of Catholicism as these influence each other, and I can only hope that I perform this task faithfully.

Of special assistance to me in this effort have been Thomas A. Hellegers, III, Donna M. Nicholas, Norwell F. Therien, Jr., and Teru Uyeyama of Prentice-Hall, Inc., as well as Margaret Chiang and Laura

Waage in the Department of Religious Studies at Seton Hall University. For their assistance in preparing and reacting to the book at various stages along the way, I am indebted to my students at Seton Hall, particularly Ralph N. Villanova, Jr., Joyce I. Lammerding, Charles Markey, and Eileen B. Dowling. Moreover, I appreciate the advice of myriad colleagues in the American academic community during the completion of this project, specifically William A. Smith, Jr. (Philosophy and American Studies), William M. Mathes and Peter M. Mitchell (History), all of Seton Hall University; Jacob Neusner (Religious Studies, Brown University); Andrew M. Greeley and William M. McCready (National Opinion Research Center, Chicago); Eugene J. Schallert, S.J. (Director, Institute for Socio-Religious Research) and John B. McGloin, S.J. (History), both of the University of San Francisco. Thanks are also due those who have long encouraged my writing, especially in this particular project, notably Terry F. Brock and Arthur N. Winter of *The National Catholic Reporter*, Robert W. Stock and Donald Johnston of *The New York Times*, Joseph R. Thomas and my colleagues on the editorial board of *The Advocate* (newspaper of the Archdiocese of Newark), as well as Thomas F. Jordan, James W. Kelly, Jr., and Robert Blair Kaiser.

Finally, my deepest thanks to those who have been closest to me throughout this project, my wife Joanne and son George.

*George Devine*

# Abbreviations

Some scholarly sources used in references for this work may be unfamiliar to some readers, although they are abbreviated as follows in conventional scholarly usage:

AAS *Acta Apostolicae Sedis*
ASS *Acta Sanctae Sedis*
CIC *Codex Iuris Canonici* (Code of Canon Law)
DS Denzinger-Schönmetzer, *Enchiridion Symbolorum*
TCT *The Church Teaches*

AAS and ASS are periodical collections of the "acts" or public utterances of the apostolic or holy see at Rome—in other words, the public statements of the Papacy. DS is a more recent edition of Denzinger's *Enchiridion* (often simply D, Denz. or Dz, and occasionally DB as distinct from DS), a collection in Latin of Church documentation from Councils, synods, the teachings of the Pope, etc. TCT is an English collection of documents selected from the earlier edition of Denzinger (DB/D/Dz/Denz.) and was compiled by the Jesuits at St. Mary's College in Kansas (Published by B. Herder Book Company, St. Louis, Mo., 1955). AAS and ASS are in libraries of note with a good theological collection, and may be found in the Catholic Periodical Index in most general libraries; Denzinger (earlier or later editions) may be found in libraries with strong theological collections, and some Catholic or scholarly oriented bookstores would have it or could locate it.

# 1

# In the World,
# But Not of It?

From the beginning, American Catholics have had a feeling of being alienated from the rest of society. Even today those of us who are relatively young can remember, directly and vicariously, a feeling of being somehow different. It was at times a great advantage to think that we had been so preferred by God as to be given the One True Faith when non-Catholics (a general term embracing atheists, Unitarians, agnostics, Lutherans, freethinkers, Jews, humanists, Baptists, pagans, Russian Orthodox, et al.) had not. At times it was also a great burden to have a series of ritual and moral obligations peculiar to the chosen. If you were Catholic, there were special things you had to do or could not do, with the understanding that it was all part of being special. Catholic emphasis on the rewards and punishments of the life hereafter thus gave rise to the popular saying that "The Catholic Church is a terrible one to live in, but a great one to die in!"

For ordinary people, death was something not to think about —a necessary, unpopular conclusion to one's life. For Catholics it was no more popular, but surely more often thought of. For citizens of "the world," death was prepared for by a few actions during one's lifetime: the making of a will, the planning of one's burial, and the like. For members of the Church, death was prepared for by *every* action of one's lifetime: daily prayers, relationships with all the persons one might encounter, ways of studying, working, and playing, loving and laughing, reading and recreation. Every aspect of a Catholic's life was a preparation for God's particular judgment of him at the end of his life, at which time he would be counted either among the blessed to be with God forever in heaven or among the damned to be cast away from him forever in hell.[1] It was thus necessary to weigh every action, every word, even every innermost thought, in such wise as to please the Almighty judge as much as possible (though it seemed that this could never be done fully) and to avoid offending him (though this, sad to say, could be done very easily).

Should a Catholic forget that the primary object of living well was to die well, the Church would seek in various ways to remind him. The first-degree initiation of the Knights of Columbus would feature a man dressed like an executioner of old, clutching a skull (recalling Hamlet's "Alas, poor Yorick") and admonishing the proselytes: *Tempus fugit; memento mori!* [2] A Catholic might often go to bed contemplating what his fate would be were he not to awaken the next morning, or he might make sure he was spiritually prepared for a sudden, unexpected death.[3]

For many American Catholics, particularly during the nadir of the immigrant out-group experience, death became almost the triumphal respite spoken of during the Middle Ages; it was the Great Equalizer, the corrector of worldly injustices. The rich Jew and the prosperous WASP (White Anglo-Saxon Protestant) would turn to dust as surely as the Polish coal miner or the Irish cop, but the Pole and the Irishman knew they would be better off in the next life if they had kept to the way of the Lord as taught through his Church. The splendor of the Requiem Mass [4]—the flowers, the incense, the vestments and statuary,

---

1 Luke 13:27.

2 In English: "Time flies; remember death!" This was part of the "secret initiation" of the Knights of Columbus, which for some time was popularly—but incorrectly— rumored to include secret oaths which would diminish the loyalty of Knights of Columbus members to the United States or enlist them in schemes to forcibly catholicize the nation at great peril to constitutional freedom of religion. This was even a minor campaign issue in 1960 when John F. Kennedy, a Knight of Columbus, was a Presidential candidate. In reality, the Knights of Columbus was but a fraternal organization for American Catholics not terribly unlike the Masons, and had an attractive insurance plan for members. It was thoroughly innocuous and still exists with a large membership today, although it does not attract anywhere near the publicity or speculation it once did.

3 The view of death in the Catholic spiritual vision is discussed in chapter 3 of my book *Transformation in Christ* (Staten Island, N.Y.: Alba House, 1972), pp. 45–56, at greater length than would be appropriate in this volume.

4 So called from the beginning of the *Introit* (Entrance Hymn) : *Requiem aeternam dona eis, Domine* ... (in English, "Eternal rest grant unto them, O Lord ...," from IV Esdras 2:34). Proper Mass formularies in the Roman Rite were commonly identified in the Latin by the first word or phrase in the *Introit;* this practice seems to have been discontinued since the vernacularization of the Roman Mass.

and the Latin hymns (like *In Paradisum*) [5]—suggested a life far different from the earthly lot of the Mexican busboy from Phoenix or the Italian garbage man from New York. There, in heaven, would be the final reward, the only place where justice could really be expected. After death came the grand finale to which all else was prelude—if only the faithful Catholic had remembered to despise and mistrust this life so as not to jeopardize the next.

For Catholics, no place was said to be "home" except heaven. This terra firma was in reality transitory. While no Catholic had the right to hasten his exit from this life (e.g., by suicide, or even by not taking proper care of himself—both violations of the Fifth Commandment), members of the Church were encouraged to look forward to death, to embrace it when it came, even to rejoice in being called early by God ("The good die young"). It was not uncommon for members of some religious orders [6] to mourn at a funeral, not for the deceased, but for themselves, because God had called a friend and not them.

In the same way, what mattered to each person was not his body but his soul. Tallness, shortness, slimness, fatness, physical beauty, plainness, and even ugliness were all insignificant. One's physical integrity or infirmity was relatively unimportant. While one was obliged to preserve one's health, an ailment could be an opportunity from God to suffer and thereby merit grace for oneself or another in the Christian community. The body was but a temporary residence for the soul. Its contents —man's intellect and will—were far more important. The outer wrappings—physical appearances—were not only trivial, but could even be traps to ensnare the faithful. Physical beauty could be a cunning deceit aimed at those trying to keep their minds and hearts in tune with only those things that were important, the things of the next life, of heaven.

The bodily life on earth was by no means incapable of providing many a source of "natural happiness," but one should never confuse it with the supernatural happiness that one would experience in eternal communion with God in heaven. So natural happiness had to be held in check, lest it was allowed to go too far. Even good things had to be restricted, lest the subsidiary or temporary pleasures of life got out of hand and distracted Catholics from the highest good,[7] the only good

---

5 Again, identified by the first phrase in the Latin text, *In Paradisum deducant te angeli...* ("Into Paradise may the angels lead you...") . This hymn, with a particularly joyous spirit, was commonly sung at the end of the Latin *Requiem* Mass; it is now often sung in the vernacular.

6 I am using "religious" here to designate members of specific religious orders although I shall state my quarrel with that nomenclature in chapter 2 of this book.

7 The idea of God as "highest good" (*Summum Bonum* in the Latin) comes especially from the philosophical and theological writings of the medieval Scholastics, notably Thomas Aquinas.

of enduring value—God himself and eternal bliss with him. For this reason Catholics denied themselves the use of meat on Fridays and other days of abstinence, fasted during penitential seasons (principally Lent, but there were other fast days throughout the liturgical year as well),[8] and during the same times usually added voluntary sacrifices (giving up smoking, drinking, movies, candy, or the like). Religious vows of chastity [9] were widely encouraged, and even married Catholics—whether or not finding periodic abstinence necessary for reasons of family limitation [10]—found themselves enjoined to consider celibacy as the model for their marital lives.[11] The limiting or even forsaking of conjugal pleasure in marriage was seen as an aid to remembering the proper scheme of priorities. As a Catholic philosopher once said to me, "The whole idea is to prevent oneself from being conned by the moment!" [12]

The "moment" in question—how long was it? As long as one's life; as long as one was sojourning on earth before going "home"; as long as one was anywhere but safe at last with God in heaven.

---

[8] "Ember Days," "Rogation Days," and vigils of certain feasts.

[9] Chastity in the sense of a religious vow means celibacy or abstinence from all sexual intercourse, as well as activities which could lead to sexual involvement (e.g., courtship or "dating," "particular friendships" with members of the opposite sex, etc.) . However, the Church has also stressed "marital chastity" as the application of the virtue of chastity in the married state (e.g., the fostering of true conjugal love, avoidance of adultery or anything that might lead to it, compliance with Church teachings regarding sexual morality in marriage, contraception, etc.) . In addition, Catholic preachers and authors have said that single persons who do not take religious vows of chastity have a sort of chastity proper to their own state in life as well (e.g., a single person may not presume the rights of married persons, but may engage in dating or courtship) .

[10] Periodic abstinence from intercourse ("the rhythm method" as it is popularly called) allows for the avoidance of intercourse when fertility is presumed likely during the menstrual cycle, and allows the resumption of intercourse when fertility is presumed impossible (especially when ovulation is past) . According to the 1968 encyclical letter *Humanae vitae* issued by Pope Paul VI, this is the only method of family limitation permissible for Catholics or indeed any men of good will who recognize, as do Catholics, the moral imperatives of natural law which all men are able to understand by their own reason. In this regard Paul VI echoes the teachings of Pius XII (1958) on rhythm, and the general context of Pius XI's encyclical letter on Christian marriage in 1930 (*Casti connubii*). During his pontificate (1958–63), Pope John XXIII made statements supporting the previous teachings of Pius XI and Pius XII. However, there has been much theological and pastoral opposition and flexible interpretation of these teachings, including Pope Paul's encyclical of 1968. See Robert G. Hoyt, ed., *The Birth Control Debate* (Kansas City, Mo.: N.C.R., 1969) and chapter 5 of this book.

[11] For one example of this, see Mary Rosera Joyce, *The Meaning of Contraception* (Staten Island, N.Y.: Alba House, 1970) .

[12] The quotation is from Vincent J. Ferrara, who was an Assistant Professor of Philosophy at Seton Hall University when he made this remark to me in 1966. I cite him because his generally liberal approach and reputation in philosophical and theological matters might underscore the widespread nature of this particular point of view at that time. In 1968 Dr. Ferrara resigned his position at Seton Hall and became Associate Professor of Philosophy at Indiana University in Pennsylvania.

To make sure that they would not be led astray from their ultimate goal or waylaid on the way "home" through this vale of tears [13] known as earthly life, it was necessary for Catholics, particularly in such a hostile land as the United States,[14] to have their own neighborhoods, schools, social clubs, hospitals, movie rating scales, insurance companies, professional societies, athletic leagues, social action groups, newspapers, paramilitary organizations,[15] publishing houses, and countless other organizations.[16] This was as recent as the late 1950s, and even the early 1960s.

What has happened since then? Anyone who is at all aware of Catholics in America realizes that their profile is now vastly different from the one just described. How does one account for this dramatic change? Popular religious journalists would tend to oversimplify the case by answering, "What happened, of course, was the Second Vatican Council!" Anyone who really understands American Catholicism would understand this as superficial analysis at best, for what happened in fact was a complex series of changes that would have taken place whether or not there had ever been a Second Vatican Council between 1962 and 1965. It is true, of course, that the Council accelerated some movements within the Church both throughout the world and in the United States particularly; and the Catholic Church has received more than its share of media coverage owing to the spectacle of the Bishops assembled in the *aula* [17] at St. Peter's in Rome and the impressive documents issued forth from their deliberations under Popes John XXIII and Paul VI.[18] Furthermore, the Council's closing date, 1965, serves as a convenient handle for the historian or student of religion interested in putting chronological tags on the phenomena which he observes and relates. For all these reasons, let us keep in mind this opinion, for it is not completely without basis in reality. As one priest remarked in 1966, about

---

[13] A popular phrase in Catholic parlance describing earthly life.

[14] The hostility of the United States toward immigrant Catholics, largely a relic today, was real enough even well into the twentieth century. See Andrew M. Greeley, *The Catholic Experience* (Garden City, N.Y.: Doubleday & Co., Inc., 1967).

[15] E.g., Catholic War Veterans. I am not referring to alleged "military" groups among American Catholics, which were once supposed to be secreting weapons for a "takeover" of the U.S. Such groups were popularly believed to exist (according to anti-Catholic propaganda) but were in fact nonexistent.

[16] See Devine, *Transformation in Christ,* chap. 5 for more detailed remarks.

[17] The large Council meeting hall St. Peter's Basilica in the Vatican. For an explanation of the internal procedures of the Second Vatican Council, see Xavier Rynne (pseud.), *Letters from Vatican City* (New York: Farrar, Straus, and Giroux, 1963) and Robert Blair Kaiser, *Pope, Council and World* (New York: Macmillan, 1963).

[18] Pope John XXIII, who convoked Vatican Council II, died between its first and second sessions, on June 3, 1963. It was up to the next pope, Paul VI, to continue the Council or not, and he did continue it through three more sessions.

six months after the formal conclusion of Vatican II, "The Council made
it all right to say out loud, in front of the whole Church, some things
that theologians had been saying among themselves for some time!" [19]
And so it was, indeed, that Paulist Press brought out a series of volumes
of recent theological research, speculation, and documentation under
the general series title *Concilium*. Although most of the material in
*Concilium* was not directly related to Vatican Council II, a great deal of
it indirectly reflected a spirit which would have developed in the Church
in any case, but which now had the import of the Council to bring it to
the center of the Catholic stage.[20]

One of the chief developments that came into full view during the
1960s was a biblical renaissance that had had its seed in the mid-
nineteenth century. During the era when the German higher criticism
school of biblical interpretation and the French rationalist movement—
contemporary with the momentous publication of Charles Darwin's *The
Origin of Species* (1859)—sent scriptural scholars back to their Bibles
and other research tools, there came to light a great deal of biblical
knowledge that had previously escaped the exegetes.[21] Deeper understandings of the primary (literal) and secondary senses of Scripture,[22]
coupled with more sophisticated research methods and sources than had
ever before existed, made it possible for scholars to enjoy a new understanding of just what the biblical authors were actually trying to set
down in a series of records which were not written as historical documents per se or science textbooks,[23] but testimonies of the religious

---

[19] Vatican II closed on December 8, 1965; this remark was made in the early
summer of 1966.

[20] I think in this connection of the education and religion columns I have done
for "The Week in Review" in *The New York Times,* where it has been my chief responsibility to portray trends. Often the *Times* editors have said to me something like,
"That's an interesting trend, and we'd like you to do a story on it for us, but it'd be so
much better if we could hang it on a specific news peg!" By way of analogy, the Second
Vatican Council provided many theologians with a "news peg."

[21] Exegetes means those involved in the detailed analysis of texts, particularly
biblical.

[22] The primary or literal sense refers to what the author intended to convey, and
the secondary sense (sometimes "spiritual sense" or in Latin *sensus plenior,* fuller sense)
to things he might have conveyed just as surely, but without necessarily consciously
intending to. See Louis Bouyer, *The Meaning of Sacred Scripture,* tr. Mary Perkins
Ryan (Notre Dame, Ind.: University of Notre Dame Press, 1958) .

[23] This does not mean that historical or scientific knowledge could never be
gleaned from biblical texts, just that this has never been their primary purpose or even
among their consciously intended purposes. They are documents of faith. Once this
fact became generally realized, the exaggerated "conflict" between Genesis and Darwin
was seen for what it was, i.e., an *"apparent* conflict" (to use the expression popular
among theologians), since Genesis never attempted a scientific explanation of creation,
but only a theological narrative of certain key points of doctrine. See Charles Hauret,
*Beginnings: Genesis and Modern Science* (Dubuque, Iowa: Priory Press, 1959), or in a
more general context, Ian G. Barbour, ed., *Issues in Science and Religion* (Englewood
Cliffs, N.J.: Prentice-Hall, Inc., 1966).

beliefs and practices of the community of faith in the Old Testament and the New Testament. This type of understanding was predicated upon a deeper appreciation of the cultures that prevailed in biblical times. No longer would it be satisfactory to translate the Old Testament from the Greek Septuagint or the New Testament from the Latin Vulgate; rather, it was necessary for biblical scholars to deal directly with the Hebrew, the *Koine* Greek, the Aramaic, and any related languages that would be helpful.[24] No longer would it be sufficient to impose on the Hebrews of 1250 B.C. the philosophical or theological categories of the western man of A.D. 1250.[25] One now attempted to walk in the very paths of the first Christians who proclaimed their belief in Jesus as Messiah and Risen Lord (*Kyrios*),[26] or of the Jews who were nomadic shepherds in Canaan a thousand years before that.[27]

Christian biblical scholars—especially the Catholics—who delved into the riches of exegesis learned that their own faith had roots far more complex and intriguing than they had suspected, which led to some most refreshing theological insights. Paramount among these was the Hebraic notion of history. In the classic Greek view of history, events occur cyclically, e.g., war, peace, prosperity, famine. Famine is eventually resolved by war, which in its turn is resolved by peace, after which comes prosperity, which degenerates into famine, and so on. The fruits of prosperity and the weapons of war may become more sophisticated, but the cycle continues. If this be the case, then man does well to live as much as possible apart from the vicissitudes of earthly life, and should indeed strive to be "other-worldly." [28] To put one's faith at all in this

---

[24] The Greek Septuagint (commonly designated in scholarly shorthand by LXX) and Latin Vulgate (commonly designated Vg or Vulg.) are indeed useful in biblical research, but no substitute for the original languages. The common (*Koine*) Greek of the NT is the original for much NT literature, unlike the LXX translation of the OT. Prior to the twentieth century, many Catholic biblical scholars did not realize or act upon this. See John J. Dougherty, *Searching the Scriptures* (Garden City, N.Y.: Doubleday & Co., Inc., 1959).

[25] A classic example of this is the interpretation by Catholic exegetes until rather recently of Exodus 3:14 as a metaphysical statement (YHWH = "I Am Who Am," unmoved mover, primary cause, etc.) when we now realize that the Hebrews of the time when the Exodus events occurred and were recorded simply did not think in such terms. See my treatment of this in *Why Read the Old Testament?* (Chicago: Claretian Publications, 1966), p. 14f.

[26] The Greek expression which occurs numerous times in the New Testament literature attributed to Paul.

[27] This fact about their lives helps us to understand images like those of the prophet Amos (himself a shepherd from the region of Tekoa), or of the famous Psalm 22 (23).

[28] See Albert Gelin, *The Key Concepts of the Old Testament,* tr. George Lamb (New York: Paulist Press Deus Books, 1963) and John Bright, *A History of Israel* (Philadelphia: Westminster Press, 1959). A more general treatment may be found in Bernhard W. Anderson, *Understanding the Old Testament* (Englewood Cliffs, N.J.: Prentice-Hall, Inc., 1957) or Paul Heinisch, *Theology of the Old Testament,* tr. William G. Heidt (Collegeville, Minn.: The Liturgical Press, 1950).

world is to guarantee bleak disillusionment. The Hellenic view of human history had a significant influence on later Christian philosophers, and so helped to form a Christian *Weltanschauung* that was most suspicious of the world. The Renaissance spirit of "All this and heaven too!" provided only a brief respite, for the agonies of division and defense which followed in the wake of the Protestant Reformation forced the Roman Church into the role of a fortress under seige and merely re-emphasized the wisdom of a viewpoint that this world was not to be trusted.[29]

Beginning in the late nineteenth century, and into the early twentieth century, Catholic biblical scholars began to drink deeply of the rich waters that flowed from the springs unearthed by their investigations. While the Holy See at Rome had cautiously encouraged these endeavors by a permission here, a tacit approval there, the *magna carta* for modern Catholic scriptural studies was to come with Pope Pius XII's encyclical letter of 1943, *Divino Afflante Spiritu*,[30] which encouraged and specified directions for further biblical research. So it was, in the later 1940s and the 1950s, that theologians came to the podiums of Catholic seminaries and colleges [31] to proclaim their new understanding of the revelations provided by the Bible, especially in the Old Testament.[32] They proclaimed for their students, their colleagues, and the Church at large the ancient Hebraic insight: *The salvation of man in this world by God takes place not* despite *human history but* through *it!*

The world was no longer to be despised as an obstacle to man's spiritual self-realization, but embraced as a vehicle for it. In fact, the very notion of "flesh" (man's earthly life) was also absolved of its pejorative implications by biblical research.[33] This meant that the world and the flesh were seen no longer as companions of the devil, but in a broad sense as sacraments for man's approaches to union with the Deity.[34]

As biblical theologians were developing this notion, it was being ap-

---

[29] Thus the "counter-reformation" spirit which prevailed in the Roman Church from the sixteenth century into the middle of the twentieth. See Charles Kohli, "A Time to Be at One," in *To Be a Man*, ed. George Devine (Englewood Cliffs, N.J.: Prentice-Hall, Inc., 1969), pp. 135–43.

[30] AAS XXXV (1943): 193–248. In English, this encyclical letter is often called "On the Most Opportune Way to Promote Biblical Studies," and was usually printed in Bibles published under Catholic auspices after World War II for textbook use and educational purposes.

[31] The wave began in European seminaries and universities, then American seminaries, and finally American colleges felt the impact around 1959–60.

[32] Partially because the Old Testament was less familiar and thus more intriguing for Catholics, partially because of Pope Pius XI's reflection that we are all "Spiritual Semites." See Devine, *Why Read the Old Testament?* p. 32.

[33] Devine, *Transformation in Christ*, pp. 49, 66.

[34] Edward Schillebeeckx, *Christ the Sacrament of the Encounter with God*, tr. Cornelius Ernst (New York: Sheed & Ward, 1963).

proached from another angle by a singular human being who was paleontologist, philosopher, poet, scientist, humanist, theologian, and priest of the Society of Jesus: Pierre Teilhard de Chardin (1881–1955). In Teilhard's view, the biological evolution heralded by Darwin would manifest its spiritual equivalent in an evolution of human socialization [35] and unification, until there evolved a final unity of matter and spirit which he called the Omega Point.[36] From Teilhard's standpoint, involvement in and with the world was nothing less than holy, for it meant participation in the unification he envisioned.

Articulating similar insights in the area of speculative theology were Europeans like Karl Rahner and Edward Schillebeeckx, both of whom had great influence on American Catholics in the 1960s. Schillebeeckx most dramatically recast the Catholic expression "sacrament," expanding its scope to transcend the traditional listing of "the seven sacraments" and embrace as sacramental all occasions for encounter with God the Father or Jesus his Son.[37] While Schillebeeckx spoke specifically in terms of Jesus as the sacrament of the encounter with God the Father, and the Church as the sacrament of the encounter with Jesus [38] (and the specific sacraments of the Church as encounters with the Divine Persons), his new approach tended to remove a set of theological horse-blinders from Catholic thinking about what could be holy and what could aid one's communion with the Trinity, to include the whole of creation among the avenues of grace. (Rahner, in various notions like that of the Church as *Ursakrament* or primordial sacrament, did very much the same.[39])

These new vistas for Catholics facing the world would all have come in due time, with or without the Second Vatican Council. But *with* the Council, as it happened, they all converged at a time when the Church throughout the world was concentrating quite seriously and consciously on a rethinking and retooling of its role and mission in the world and when the American Catholic was emerging from the insecurity of the immigrant ghetto to first-class membership in all phases of U.S. society.[40]

Thus a new rationale developed for a Catholic Church—an *American*

---

35 Pierre Teilhard de Chardin, *The Future of Man,* tr. Norman Denny (Evanston, Ill.: Harper & Row, 1964), especially chap. 3, "The Grand Option."

36 Pierre Teilhard de Chardin, *The Phenomenon of Man,* tr. Norman Denny (Evanston, Ill.: Harper & Row, 1959).

37 Schillebeeckx, *Christ the Sacrament of the Encounter with God,* chaps. 1 and 2.

38 Devine, *Transformation in Christ,* chap. 3.

39 Karl Rahner, *The Church and the Sacraments,* tr. W.J. O'Hara, *Quaestiones Disputatae* Series No. II (New York: Herder & Herder, 1963). Also see his *Nature and Grace,* tr. Dinah Wharton (London: Sheed & Ward, 1963), especially chaps. 1, 2, 3, and 5.

40 See Andrew M. Greeley, *The Catholic Experience,* and Devine, *Transformation in Christ,* chap. 2.

Catholic Church—that would pride itself, not on its being different, but on its fitting into the general scheme of things. Catholics in America remained members of the City of God, but no longer in opposition to citizenship in the "secular city." American Catholics who were wont to envision themselves at war with the motion picture industry (particularly during the heyday of the Legion of Decency) now tended to embrace the celluloid medium and celebrate it in courses on "theology of film," leaving censorship of movies pretty much in the hands of the industry itself (under the aegis of the MPAA).[41] Catholics who feared that the "secular press" could not give fair coverage to Catholic matters and might taint secular news with amoral viewpoints now began eschewing some of the traditional periodicals of the ghetto[42] and picking up *The New York Times,* whose pages began to feature distinguished Catholic writers previously found only in publications like *America, Commonweal,* and the Catholic diocesan weeklies.[43] Catholics who had battled vigorously for separate school systems, from nursery school through postdoctoral studies,

---

[41] The Legion of Decency afforded Catholics a complex system of movie ratings in terms of their moral objectionability or lack of it, and was widely adhered to by lay Catholics despite its lack of genuine binding ecclesiastical authority (see *Transformation in Christ,* pp. 108, 115). By the mid-1960s, the Legion's emphasis had become more positive, as had its title, which was changed to the National Catholic Office for Motion Pictures (NCOMP). Its influence on film ratings became somewhat diminished by the G, PG, M, R, and X designations of the Motion Picture Association of America, although many religious spokesmen, including Catholics inside and outside of NCOMP, were to lament the laxity which followed the religious groups' resolution to encourage "self-regulation" by the movie industry.

[42] While some traditional Catholic magazines either changed outright (e.g., *St. Jude* to *U.S. Catholic*) or died on the vine, there was a strong attachment to some conservative publications like *The Wanderer.* Also, some of the better moderate and progressive journals like *America, The Critic,* and *The Commonweal* survived, and the Kansas City (diocesan) *Reporter* gained international status for its independent religious journalism and became *The National Catholic Reporter.* Interestingly enough, the *N.C.R.*'s editor and publisher, Donald J. Thorman, had at one time been part of a group which had considered a Catholic daily. (See Garry Wills, "A Farewell (Quite Fond) to the Catholic Liberal," in a clever "Catholic Nostalgia" issue of *The Critic* 29:3 (January–February 1971), 14–22. In 1970, Thorman became both publisher and editor, winning a board of directors showdown with editor Robert G. Hoyt, who wanted to abandon much of *N.C.R.*'s intramural ecclesiastical coverage. Thorman's point of view (supported by people like Andrew M. Greeley) was that because the paper could do this particular job better than anyone else, that was its *raison d'être;* he saw no point in trying to win back progressives who had opted out of the Church and would not read a "Catholic" paper anyway, but would prefer the resources of other journals like *The New York Review of Books,* and others.

[43] I am thinking here of writers like Andrew M. Greeley, Wilfrid Sheed, Garry Wills, and John Cogley, who for a time served as religion correspondent for *The New York Times.* Father Greeley, however, felt that a good Catholic paper like *The National Catholic Reporter* could still do its particular job better than *The New York Times.*

began to consider quite favorably the offerings of public education agencies and to move into leadership positions in the effort to improve public education (previously the "competition").

The emergence of Catholics into every aspect of mainstream American life made it otiose for Catholic newspapers to point out the number of municipal and state officials, movie stars, athletes, or other prominent personages who represented the Catholic minority. Various concerns no longer tended to employ "house Catholics." [44]

One of the feelings that lay behind this shift was that the Catholic experience in America was no longer simply an immigrant experience. Catholics were no longer the oppressed minority they had been in the nineteenth and early twentieth centuries. One man, early in the 1960s, had even broken down the last vestiges of religious bigotry on his way into the White House.[45] It was no longer necessary for Catholics to huddle together in fear of the world outside, anxiously clamoring for the political, economic, educational, as well as spiritual and moral protection of the Catholic subculture. The Irish-Catholic, Polish-Catholic, and Italian-Catholic ghetto neighborhoods of the big cities were beginning to depopulate as more and more American Catholics joined the middle class, staking their claims on suburbia.[46]

In an era when religious divisions appeared to be on the wane, American Christians in general (and some Jews as well, remembering how their people had profited from the secularization of many European societies) [47] began to celebrate the values and opportunities of the "secular city." [48] Specifically religious institutions needed to be maintained only minimally, and men of faith were free, even exhorted, to drink deeply of the common secular experience. While the coming of age of American immigrant Catholicism was the social phenomenon that made this new participation in secular life possible for the Catholic populace of the

---

[44] Analogous to Geraldo Rivera's description of himself as "house Puerto Rican" at WABC-TV in New York. See *New York* 5:32 (August 7, 1972), 56.

[45] Greeley, *The Catholic Experience,* pp. 280–314.

[46] See Andrew M. Greeley's article on the experience of the Irish-American Catholics who moved to suburbia in the mid-twentieth century and what he considers to be the communally and personally disintegrating effects of the move, "The Last of the American Irish Fade Away," *The New York Times Magazine* (March 14, 1971), pp. 32ff.

[47] I have in mind here Rabbi Eugene Borowitz's analyses of this subject. Also see Jacob Neusner, *Judaism in the Secular Age* (New York: KTAV Publishing House, Inc., 1970).

[48] This phrase became famous in the mid-1960s through the writings of Harvey Cox, who seems to have changed his outlook a bit in the waning years of that decade. See Harvey Cox, *The Secular City* (New York: The MacMillan Company, 1965) and *Feast of Fools* (Cambridge: Harvard University Press, 1969).

United States, there had to be an intellectual and theological foundation for it as well, if newly mobile Catholics were to feel comfortable in their coming-out in American society.

The very insights we have just surveyed made their way to American Catholics through theologians, retreat masters, chaplains, professors, confessors, secondary and elementary school teachers, Catholic publications, CCD courses,[49] and so on. Not that these sources repeated the theological rationale in toto; what was transmitted, in each case, was a digest of appropriate dimensions for the specific audiences and circumstances in question. In many instances, both transmitters and receivers were unfamiliar with technical theological argot or with exotic names like Schillebeeckx and others. But the message throughout was this: Catholics needed no longer fear or fight the world, but could now immerse themselves in it as a manifestation of the saving love of Christ, both receiving from, and giving to, the world the salvific grace of the Word who became flesh.[50] This was surely the thrust of the Second Vatican Council and also of Pope Paul VI's encyclical letter of 1964, *Ecclesiam Suam*.[51] And this spirit manifested itself through nuns who chose secular clothing in place of habits,[52] a Jesuit priest who ran for Congress (and was elected), religious-order members who became lawyers, psychologists, social workers, and movie directors,[53] and even a Supreme Pontiff who rode a jet plane to say Mass in a baseball stadium adjacent to the IRT el tracks in the Bronx.[54]

The rush of Catholics to embrace the world anew was a bit dizzying; it took on proportions that were almost extreme. This was understandable, though, in light of the suspicion with which the Church had viewed

---

49 CCD: Confraternity of Christian Doctrine, which conducts religious education classes for elementary and secondary school students who attend nonparochial schools, in their respective Catholic parishes or dioceses. CCD also conducts some adult education and other programs as well.

50 The idea implied here is that Jesus took unto himself all dimensions of the human situation, rendering it no longer contemptible, but utterly redeemable. See Hebrews 4:15, John 1:14, and Devine, *Transformation in Christ*, chap. 3.

51 AAS LIX (1964), 609–59.

52 For one survey of change in religious-order life in the American Church, see Kenneth Woodward, et al., "The New U.S. Nun: A Joyous Revolution," *Newsweek* 70:26 (December 25, 1967), 45ff.

53 Examples of these abound: Father Robert Drinan, S.J. (D.-Mass.); Rev. Eugene C. Kennedy, M.M., psychologist; innumerable religious social workers like Sister Kathleen Gallagher, O.P.; cinema director Rev. William Hogan, S.J., multimedia Dominican priests Anthony Shillaci and Blaise Schauer, and others.

54 This reference, of course, is to Pope Paul VI's Mass for Peace at Yankee Stadium in New York on October 4, 1965, in conjunction with his visit earlier that day to the United Nations headquarters.

the secular order until the early and mid-1960s. It should not have been altogether surprising to see small communities of "liberated" Catholics celebrate the Mass liturgy in apartments rather than in sanctuaries of churches, priests wearing secular street clothes instead of liturgical vestments, or attending nuns (also in mufti) identifying themselves as "Pat" (for Sister Patricia) or "Connie" (for Sister Constance). In addition, specially prepared hosts and sacramental altar wine were forsaken in favor of large loaves of leavened bread (in San Francisco sourdough French bread was used) and the fruit of the secular vine (no longer Christian Brothers or Novitiate, now sometimes even Manischewitz). To Catholics caught up in this new spirit, nothing was unholy, nothing was profane; thus, logically, it became most difficult to identify anything as specially sacred.[55]

One of the chief ramifications of this new worldview for Catholics was the abandonment of the view that Catholic life was centered in the salvation of one's own individual soul. Instead, it was stressed that man must not only attend to his material needs as well as his spiritual needs, but that neither could an individual soul nor an individual body-person [56] find salvation in isolation. Like the salvation that came to Israel in the Old Covenant,[57] the salvation that came to man in the New Covenant of Jesus was social by nature. This insight was by no means new; it was as old as the Gospel message itself and had been emphasized for almost a century in the "social encyclicals" of Popes Leo XIII, Pius XI, John XXIII, and Paul VI.[58] But its previous emphasis had been against a background of Catholic isolationism, of condescension toward those sojourners in the world who were not safely inside the Catholic fortress. Now, when the *magisterium* [59] of the Church called on Catholics to take seriously the social and economic problems of the day, the appeal hit home more readily, as did the notion that *all* men are entitled to social

---

[55] Consider this especially in light of the Hebrew roots for our English term "holy," implying something cut off or segregated with a special meaning or function. See Devine, *Transformation in Christ*, pp. 97–98.

[56] I am here reflecting terms as popularized by Merleau-Ponty. See Mary-Rose Barral, *Merleau-Ponty: The Role of the Body-Subject in Interpersonal Relations* (Pittsburgh: Duquesne University Press, 1965).

[57] Devine, *Why Read the Old Testament?* Again, note the important OT influence on contemporary Catholic theology.

[58] See Charles E. Curran's analysis of the development of "Roman Catholic Social Ethics" in *That They May Live: Theological Reflections on the Quality of Life,* ed. George Devine (Staten Island, N.Y.: Alba House, 1972).

[59] *Magisterium:* the official teaching of the Church (not always specifically papal, and seldom claiming infallibility).

justice, not only those who perceive and accept the truth of the Catholic faith.[60]

For a time, at least, this made for a dramatic upswing in Catholic involvement in social, economic, and political affairs. The Kennedy Brothers certainly helped characterize the new Catholic view of politics.[61] No longer a dirty business entered into so as to protect one's own, politics now became a semiholy vocation taken up to right wrongs and minister to those in need. It now became fashionable for the Irish or Italian Catholic to engage in politics when it was no longer just a matter of taking care of his own *paisani* or "the boys from home." There began to arise American Catholic politicians who presented less and less the image of one of the downtrodden speaking for his fellows, and more and more that of the fortunate American nobly aiding the less fortunate. (R. Sargent Shriver, Eugene J. McCarthy, Edmund S. Muskie, and Joseph L. Alioto have all to some extent conformed to this image, or tried to, more than such "old pols" as Richard J. Daley, Hugh J. Addonizio, and others.) It even became quite acceptable for some clergymen in the Church to seek political office. Some did this successfully: Father Drinan of Massachusetts is the best example, but there are others. We shall see, however, that Father Reed of San Francisco, and also Father Lawlor of Chicago, began to introduce into the American Catholic scene a strange mix of the new theology and politics with the old. By the end of the 1960s, the initial enthusiasm that had greeted the insights of the era had been dampened by the events of what John Cogley called "the decade of disillusionment," [62] and this was to have profound implications for the Catholic in America as the 1970s began.

The "conservative" element in the American Church had not been heard from very much in the euphoric days right around the time of the Council. At a time when new things for Catholics to say and do were coming on the scene, they were predictably saying and doing nothing they had not said or done before. That the right-wing element in the Church spoke in opposition to the new trends attracted virtually no attention, for they had been heard from for so long and had had more than their day in court. It was time now for another sector in the Church to be listened to.

---

60 Thus we see why it is important that Pope John XXIII's 1963 encyclical *Pacem in Terris* ("Peace on Earth") was addressed not to the Church through his brother bishops, as is typically the way of encyclical letters, but "to all men of good will." See Curran, in *That They May Live.*

61 Greeley, *The Catholic Experience.*

62 Devine, *Transformation in Christ*, chaps. 1 and 8.

Even the more articulate conservatives in the Church, like William
E. Buckley, Jr., were being considered out of it in the mid-1960s and
were being virtually ostracized from American Catholic intellectual circles
because they expressed loud reservations about current trends in liturgy,
the social apostolate, and other facets of Catholic life.[63] At the same time,
former Catholic intellectual heroes abroad, like Jacques Maritain in
France, Graham Greene, Evelyn Waugh in England, and others, were
being taken off their pedestals because they opposed the vernacularization of the Latin liturgy.[64] During the mid-1960s, it was terribly out of
fashion to say "Holy Ghost" rather than "Holy Spirit," let alone favor
retention of Latin, the Gregorian Chant, or incense during the Mass.[65]
Likewise, it was unacceptable to prefer English translations of the liturgical texts which represented anything other than the modern language
(i.e., no "thee-thy-thou").[66] The spirit of modernization went even further:
no longer was there a special language that was sacred for worship, no
longer a special setting or a special type of garb, and thus, no longer
special music. The organ, no more the only sacred instrument for worship,
gave way to the "folk Mass." [67] Young Catholic Americans began to
worship with guitar, banjo, and tambourine, utilizing lyrics which reflected the maudlin words that characterized the hymns of Catholic wor-

---

[63] In 1966 I was one of the faculty members who vigorously—and unsuccessfully
—opposed the granting of an honorary doctorate to Mr. Buckley at the Commence-
ment of Seton Hall University, on the grounds that "his thinking is out of touch
with the modern Church and a bad example for the Archdiocesan University to be
putting before the Catholic populace." In looking back, I realize that I was terribly
intolerant.

[64] See David Lodge, "The Arrogance of Evelyn Waugh," *The Critic* 30 (May–
June, 1972), 62–70.

[65] "Holy Ghost" was considered a deathly expression, not only by the teachers
of religion to children, but also by linguists who felt that in modern English "spirit"
better represented what was meant by the German *Geist.*

[66] There was some tension in the initial translation of the Mass texts into English,
in that the scriptural lessons were translated by scholars favoring modern English,
and the sequences (chants like *Veni, Sancte Spiritus,* and *Dies Irae,* the latter since
de-emphasized) by those favoring archaic translations.

[67] The chief practitioners of the folk Mass in this country then were Ray Repp
(published by F.E.L. Church Publications in Los Angeles), Joe Wise, and Sebastian
Temple (both published by World Library of Sacred Music in Cincinnati). Two popular
single hymns, "They'll Know We Are Christians by Our Love" by Peter Scholtes
and "Sons of God" by James Theim, were published by F.E.L. Before the folk Mass
itself really developed, Clarence Joseph Rivers developed "The American Mass Program," a blending of simple liturgical melodies in common usage with Black American
musical patterns, in 1964 (published by WLSM). Of course there were many other
sources of liturgical folk Mass music in the late 1960s.

ship a century before,[68] or sometimes even borrowing their Mass hymns from the nearest jukebox.[69]

This by itself would have been enough to set off a reaction in conservative Catholic circles, but other things began to happen as well. The "secular saints" of the day lost popularity when their programs began to fail and some were even assassinated.[70] The popular Catholic emphasis on racial justice in the early 1960s began to ebb when riots broke out in heavily Catholic cities like Newark in the late 1960s, and the defensive white vigilantes were recruited from largely Catholic constituencies.[71] The Catholics in America, who had always taken care to demonstrate their unswerving patriotism, were now confounded by fellow Catholics who opposed Government policies in Vietnam, and by nuns and priests, who demonstrated outside draft centers and cathedrals or stood trial for conspiracy against the Government.[72]

Many conservative American Catholics began to view the folk-singing youths at Mass as sacrilegious, to say nothing of traitorous. They had no use for the priests who encouraged the new hang-loose liturgies, or who exhibited too great an interest in "secular" affairs. "The priests should mind their business and stay out of politics! They belong in the pulpits and not in the streets!" came the cries from the Catholic right, which by the end of the 1960s had a bit of contemporary history to back up its more cautious approaches. The conservatives were quick to observe that priests who became too interested in "secular matters" like politics, work with addicts, or civil rights tended to "lose their vocations," usually getting married, and often to nuns who had gone astray by the same route.[73]

Just as "the forgotten Americans" began to come to the fore during and after the election of 1968,[74] so did "the forgotten Catholics." They

---

[68] "Take Our Bread," for example, was essentially of the same genre as "O Lord I Am Not Worthy." See remarks on this subject in my column on liturgical music which appeared monthly in the *Topic* magazine section of *The Advocate* (Newark, N.J.), 1967–70.

[69] Some popular songs adapted for folk Mass use in the late 1960s were "Sounds of Silence" (Simon and Garfunkel), "The Impossible Dream" (from *Man of La Mancha*), "Somewhere, My Love" (from the score of the film *Doctor Zhivago*).

[70] Devine, *Transformation in Christ,* chap. 1.

[71] The Vailsburg Security Patrol in the West Ward of Newark recruited a heavy Irish-Catholic and Italian-Catholic membership, as did the "vigilantes" of Anthony Imperiale in that city's North Ward.

[72] E.g., the Berrigan Brothers, and others.

[73] This assumption was generally a gross and erroneous oversimplification, as will be discussed in chapter 2.

[74] I have in mind the popular support gained by Spiro T. Agnew, and also the mysterious shift of voter support from the slain Robert F. Kennedy to George C. Wallace.

began utilizing with great selectivity some of the Church's new poltical tactics of "due process" and "collegiality," introduced in the wake of Vatican II, for their own causes. With their power as subscribers and advertisers they kept *The Wanderer* going, as well as the annual Wanderer Forum,[75] and supported new conservative pressure groups within the Catholic subculture like The Roman Forum, Catholics United for the Faith, and *Una Voce*.[76] They subscribed to new conservative Catholic journals like *Triumph* and *Catholic Currents*,[77] and shunned those Catholic periodicals like *Catholic World*, which expressed liberal views.[78] They rejoiced in the diminishing circulation of *The National Catholic Reporter*,[79] and the demise of the "modernized" *Ave Maria*.[80] In the diocese of Fresno, in California, they managed to effect the shutdown of a diocesan paper that sympathized with Cesar Chavez against the agricultural interests in that region,[81] using Chavez's very tactic of economic boycott. On the liturgical scene, they rallied around Father Gommar dePauw in his Ave Maria chapel, at the headquarters of the Catholic Traditionalist Movement in Westbury, Long Island,[82] and petitioned a number of dioceses for a certain minimum number of Masses, not only celebrated in Latin, but even according to the Tridentine formula superseded by Paul VI's new *Ordo Missae*.[83] In the educational arena, they rejected the new catechistic trends that spoke of love and openness rather than obligation and sin, and they occasioned a surprising return to popularity of the Baltimore Catechism.[84] In some places they

------

[75] *The Wanderer*, a lay-operated Catholic weekly out of the Midwest, sponsors an annual convention called the Wanderer Forum.

[76] *Una Voce* is a traditionalist organization calling for the return of Latin and Gregorian Chants in the liturgy. In English, it means a movement for the Church to express itself in worship with one voice.

[77] Both under the aegis of William F. Buckley, Jr.'s brother-in-law, L. Brent Bozell, in Washington. The two have been rumored to be at odds over Mr. Bozell's "going too far" in opposing abortion, to the point where Mr. Bozell allegedly sponsored a hospital-storming group called the "Sons of Thunder" in Washington.

[78] Largely owing to the anti-Vietnam stance of editor Rev. John Sheerin, C.S.P.

[79] See footnotes 42 and 43.

[80] In 1970 the magazine changed its name to *A.D. 1970*, then folded.

[81] The demise of *The Central California Register* took place in 1972. Bishop Hugh A. Donohoe would not alter his position, and could not reinstate the paper. The editor, Gerard E. Sherry, took a vacant editorship at *The Monitor*, the archdiocesan weekly in San Francisco.

[82] There seems some question as to Father dePauw's precise Church status, but the general impression is that he is in good standing.

[83] The new "Order of the Mass" implemented in 1970, which simplified and modernized the *Ordo Missae* that had obtained since the Council of Trent in the sixteenth century.

[84] The traditional question-and-answer religious instruction book which began to be replaced by "updated" catechistic religion texts in the mid-1960s.

even established their own Catholic schools independent of parish and diocesan officials to ensure the traditional teaching of the Catholic faith to their young.[85]

In some instances members of the Catholic right had been there all along, merely ignored while the reformers had their mid-1960s heyday. In many other cases they had been moderate Catholics (sometimes even liberals) who had found the religious and secular modernizations of the 1960s disappointing and alarming. Whatever their origins, by the early 1970s they were surely being heard from. Some even took active political stands by campaigning against busing with Father Reed who was running for the San Francisco Board of Education, by trying to preserve an all-white enclave on Chicago's South Side with Father Lawlor as a municipal candidate, and even by attempting an unlikely *modus vivendi* between Italians and Puerto Ricans when they supported Father Gigante for Congressional election in New York's gerrymandered "Triborough District."[86] Even when their efforts did not enjoy the strength of numbers (as was sometimes the case at the polls), they were vocal indeed, and the Catholic conservatives who had been silenced in the middle of the 1960s were silent no more.

This resulted by the early 1970s in an American Catholic Church badly torn asunder by frustration, suspicion, and fear. Every participant in the life of the Church in the United States during these times felt the casualties that the infighting had inflicted: a diminution in religious-order memberships and vocations to the priesthood; an exodus of clergy from the active ministry; a dramatic falling-off of church attendance, especially among the young; a crisis of confidence in Catholic education; a profound spiritual and moral anxiety brought about by a decade of sudden and massive alteration in even the smallest facets of a Catholic life style that no one had expected to change; and a suprisingly turbulent reaction to unpopular utterances by the Pope on topics ranging from the eucharistic presence of Christ[87] to contraception[88] and priestly celibacy.[89]

For conservatives in the Church, the only hopeful direction to go was backward, to the safer, more stable religious patterns of the 1950s and before, in order to stem the tide of such contemporary chaos. For progres-

---

85 Holy Innocents School in Kinnelon, New Jersey, where parents travel up to fifty miles a day to deliver and pick up their children, is one example. The diocese of Paterson, in which it is located, appears to have taken a "hands-off" position.

86 So called because it encompasses parts of Manhattan, Queens, and the Bronx, near the Triborough Bridge. Father Gigante represented various constituencies, including Italian East Harlem, in his district. He has since been seated on the New York City Council.

87 *Mysterium fidei*, AAS LVII (1965), 753ff.

88 *Humanae vitae*, AAS LX (1968), 481–503.

89 *Sacerdotalis caelibatus*, AAS LIX (1967), 657–97.

sives, the same signs seemed to point to an exodus from the institutional Church, for though they felt some battles had been won, they appeared to be losing the war. At first, the exodus took the form of dramatic exits from the priesthood by revered clerical leaders like Bernard Cooke,[90] then religious personages like Bishop Shannon left the ecclesiastical scene altogether; [91] later it appeared more and more Catholics were opting out of Church involvement, while seeming to maintain vestiges of it, seeking their fortunes in the *saeculum* [92] and preserving at most only minimal ties to their Catholic heritage and community.[93] For the bulk of American Catholics—neither conservative nor stanchly progressive—it was all confusing and disheartening, and caused many to feel more despair than hope, more uncertainty than solace in the life of the Church in contemporary America. Perhaps the most confused and beleaguered of all in the American Church were those charged with leading it.

---

[90] Cooke had been chairman of the theology faculty at Marquette University; he is now laicized, and has become a professor of religion at Windsor University in Ontario.

[91] James Shannon, formerly Auxiliary Bishop of Minneapolis–St. Paul, was reported to have begun studies in law.

[92] Time and place, from which comes our English term *secular*.

[93] In many cases this means minimal sacramental participation and selective doctrinal and moral conformity, not terribly unlike some of the anticlericalism that has been chronicled in certain European localities over the past century and longer.

# 2

# A Holy Nation,
# A Royal Priesthood

"Why do we tip our hat to a priest? Why do we call him Father?" These are the words of John Redmond, composer of a series of catechistic songs [1] under the title *The Seven Sacraments*. His questions answered themselves: "He is like Christ, and how do we know? Holy Orders made him so!" The Redmond songs,[2] released just before the era of Vatican II, never managed to make their desired impact on the American Catholic populace. Instead, they were criticized for their saccharine lyrics and honky-tonk musical style. But given a different musical vehicle, they might well have gained great popularity, for what they expressed well typified the faith and practice of American Catholics up until and during the early 1960s. Among the various ditties portraying the Sacraments of the Church, "Why Do We Tip Our Hat to a Priest?" was a pivotal song in the Redmond collection because it identified the chief mediator of sacramental presence and effect, the ordained priest. Without needing to explore such theological concepts as *potestas ordines*

---

1 Catechistic means pertaining to religious instruction, that is, meant to engender or enhance religious faith and practice, in this case, to instruct young Catholics about the import of the Seven Sacraments. The term *catechetical* is also used.

2 As they came to be called, as with another popular phenomenon of the time, "The Gelineau Psalms," generally preferred by Catholics for their more subtle and majestic style of popular song.

and *potestas iurisdictionis* [3] or *ex opere operato* and *ex opere operantis*,[4] Redmond summed it up succinctly enough: "In life's great moments, Father will be there!"

The "great moments," to be sure, were the occasions for reception of the Seven Sacraments. Some of these could be received only once (Baptism, Confirmation), others only by some, depending on their state in life (Holy Orders, Matrimony); others could be received numerous times in a Catholic life, although the first time would be of special significance (Penance, Holy Eucharist); [5] two were meant to be administered by a bishop (Confirmation, Holy Orders),[6] one depending on need (Extreme Unction, or Anointing of the Sick) and one (Matrimony) by the lay recipients themselves. The frequency and form of the sacraments notwithstanding, a parish priest would almost always be on hand in one capacity or another—performing the sacramental rite, officiating at it, witnessing it, or assisting at it, as a special mediator between the Persons of the Blessed Trinity and the believing Church for which Father, Son, and Holy Spirit would be sacramentally present.

Catholic sacramental theology in practice lends strong emphasis to the Incarnation, the dogma that Jesus took on all dimensions of human existence and experience (excepting sin) [7] in becoming man. Therefore, it makes sense that matter be a medium for the sacraments: the bread and wine of the Eucharist, the human sexual encounter of Matrimony, the water of Baptism, and the oil of anointing.[8] For Catholics, the sacraments are not divorced or set apart from life in some ethereal or nonphysical way; rather, they are right in the middle of human experience. For this reason there would be many situations and objects which, even though not officially numbered among the Seven Sacraments or codified in the liturgy,[9] would be part and parcel of Catholic worship. A variety of prayers, practices, devotions, and objects for veneration and inspiration (often called "sacramentals") radiated from the core of the

---

[3] Power of orders and power of jurisdiction; see Charles Journet, *The Church of the Word Incarnate,* tr. A.H.C. Downes (New York: Sheed & Ward, 1955), Vol. 1 ("Apostolic Hierarchy").

[4] DS 3846.

[5] There is some tendency today to de-emphasize a child's (or adult convert's) first confession or first Holy Communion, but the traditional practice is to lend special emphasis to the first reception of each of these sacraments.

[6] CIC, Can. 782.

[7] John 1:14; Heb. 14:7.

[8] Oil is used in the sacrament now called Anointing of the Sick, or formerly Extreme Unction, as well as in some others.

[9] Liturgy here meaning the official public worship of the Church. Some devotions are purely private and personal. Some others are public but not truly official, and are thus called paraliturgical.

official sacramental worship of the Church, and Father would also participate in and bless these. If not officially, he was often present informally; if not in the flesh, at least through his spiritual presence and psychological influence. Catholics did not need a priest on hand in order to venerate statues or pictures of Jesus, the Blessed Virgin, or the Saints in their homes, but such objects were usually blessed by a priest.[10] Lay members of the Church did not need to have a cleric present in order to carry out the tradition of "blessing themselves" or making the Sign of the Cross [11] with holy water, but to be truly a sacramental, the water had to undergo a ritual at the hands of the priest.[12] The private prayers people said as part of their personal devotional lives, and a supplement to liturgical worship needed no sacerdotal presence, but they were usually written or compiled in prayerbooks by priests, and bore the ecclesiastical approval of clerical authorities.[13]

In the subculture that American Catholics had built, it would be difficult to imagine any event, even a seemingly "secular" one, taking place without Father there. Father would bless a new home or new car. He would often hand out the report cards in the parochial school while the teacher or principal (usually a nun) looked on somewhat nervously. He would lead the school athletic teams in prayer before a game, and remind the boys to bless themselves before approaching the batter's box or the free-throw line. At civic or social luncheons and banquets, Father would normally be asked to say grace. In myriad human situations, his advice, his consolation, and his presence would be sought and trusted. If a boy got into trouble with the law, at school, or with a girl; if somebody out of luck needed a home or a meal or a job; if a man was headed for the bottle or a marriage was headed for the rocks, Father was the one to see.

In the immigrant ghettos of Catholic America, the priest became even

---

[10] This was a devotional practice which did not enhance the value of the object used as an aid in prayer. Indeed, Catholic regulations have long prohibited the fixing of a price on a religious article because of its having been blessed, and thus the practice has been that such objects when offered for sale are not blessed.

[11] The right hand is touched to the forehead, chest, left shoulder, and right shoulder as the individual prays, "In the name of the Father/and of the Son/and of the Holy Spirit. Amen." In the Eastern Rites, the order of the left and right shoulders is reversed, and three fingers of the right hand are used, to signify the Three Persons of the Blessed Trinity.

[12] Holy water, according to the *Maryknoll Catholic Dictionary,* comp. Albert J. Nevins (New York: Grosset & Dunlap Dimensions Books, 1965), p. 275, is "A sacramental water blessed by a priest to impart God's blessing on those who use it."

[13] This is the approval of a diocesan censor deputized to read the work in question and make sure it contained no violations of Catholic dogma or moral teaching, and the official order of the Ordinary (Bishop) of the place in question to let it be printed (*Imprimatur*).

more important. He was a political leader on the local level, legal adviser, front-runner for his people through the mazes of municipal bureaucracy, chief teacher, and cultural pacesetter. For all their verisimilitude, the Bing Crosby movies [14] never captured (and perhaps never could) the multifaceted influence of the priest in an American Catholic community. Unlike the Hollywood version, the typical American cleric did not look like a matinee idol, could not sing his way through a *Missa Cantata* without difficulty,[15] and would not be destined for some athletic hall of fame had it not been for his priestly vocation. But he was a man from among the people who would be at once taken from their lives and immersed in them, called upon to strike a delicate balance between the practical needs of his people politically, educationally, and economically and the moral and spiritual priorities of a kingdom not of this world.[16] His hours were often long and his work arduous if he were in the least conscientious, and there was always more to be done. Moreover, his life was fraught with a host of dangers. Excessive involvement in the secular life would make him a political meddler, a Father Coughlin.[17] Excessive aloofness could render him irrelevant and impotent. All work and no play would not only make Father Jack a dull boy, but could cause him to snap, to veer either in the direction of compromising his vow of celibacy, or toward that legendary curse of the priesthood, alcoholism. Too much self-indulgence, on the other hand, might produce a pot-bellied and opulent country club cleric, who could wield a golf club more adeptly than the sacred objects of worship, and the Church could ill afford even a few such priests.

The Catholic priest, like his lay counterpart, found life full of traps; but for the priest, they could multiply. Obedience to authority (unlike that found in a job in "the world") had to be unswerving, even in the fact of a senile pastor or a cantankerous superior. The frustration of spending years of one's life with potentials untapped or skills untried was often possible, owing to the vicissitudes of ecclesiastical politics. Obligations toward parents (who had "given up a son") could be stronger than those felt by married sons and daughters, yet religious orders or dioceses would often assign personnel deliberately separating them from families "as a test of vocation." Moreover, the priest had to watch his

---

[14] *Going My Way* (1944) and *The Bells of St. Mary's* (1945), both released by Paramount Pictures, in which Crosby played Father O'Malley, who saved more than one parish from disaster by his unique talents and charms.

[15] *Missa Cantata* is a sung Mass or "high Mass," with which the average priest would doubtless experience at least some difficulty. By way of contrast, Crosby's Father O'Malley sang at the drop of a biretta.

[16] John 18:36.

[17] Sheldon Marcus, *Father Coughlin: The Tumultuous Life of the Priest of the Little Flower* (New York: Little, Brown and Co., 1973).

every move. He could not relax over a drink with the fellows in the neighborhood tavern, as could any other man of the parish. In many major cities, he could not attend legitimate theater, lest he cause a scandal by patronizing shows with "scanty" costumes, "off-color" dialogue, or "suggestive" material. Even the movies he chose had to conform to the recommendations of the Legion of Decency.[18] And of course, with whom could he really socialize and play except fellow clerics?

A life of this sort either required *or produced* special discipline, and came to be associated with a particular type of strength to which other members of the community barely dreamed of aspiring. Through it all, for the priest, was the consolation that it was all necessary for the salvation of mankind in the Kingdom of Christ, and that this salvation was actually forthcoming.

The rigors of clerical life and the good done by the priest for the community were such that lay people commonly stood in awe of their clergy, sometimes overlooking their minor (or even major) faults while giving full stress to their virtues. Usually everyone laughed just a little bit harder at a joke of Father's, doled a little more food onto Father's plate (he needed it, after all), or listened with special attention and respect when Father began to speak, even if he was only commenting on the day's baseball scores. Yet at the same time, many who drank would look askance if Father took a taste of liquor, many who regularly cursed might cluck their tongues if Father were heard to mutter "damn" or "hell" (outside a properly theological context), and millions of married Catholics would be shocked at the vaguest suggestion of Father's engaging in the sort of sexual experience that was a sacramental part of their own lives.

Within the subculture of Catholic America, as in other countries, the cleric was assigned the hardest job and sometimes the highest wage. The priest (and in turn the religious brother or sister) would often get to live in a nice, comfortable place and receive education, lifetime support, and security from the community, in addition to the love, respect, and obedience of countless Catholics. The clerics or religious-order members were entrusted with the ownership and management of vast areas of land, hospital complexes, sizable housing facilities, a network of printed-media facilities known as "the Catholic press," and an educational empire huge and variegated enough to stagger the imagination. To the "religious" and clergy of the Roman Catholic Church in America in different orders and dioceses were given mansions, farms, palaces, skyscrapers, estates, campuses, and millions of dollars in stocks, bonds, insurance policies, deeds, and cash. Occasionally part of this wealth was used for

---

18 The Legion of Decency is described in chapter 1, fn. 41.

the comforts of the recipients, whereas many lay people had little chance of earning such a living. But more typically, the priests, nuns, and religious brothers rendered to the community at large an account of their stewardship in terms of children educated, sick cared for, and facilities built or maintained for constructive service.

In truth, the dominance in earlier American Catholic life of religious-order members and clerics was something of a stopgap situation. Entrance into the seminary, abbey, or convent was for many the only way to education and ascendancy in the pyramid of the subculture.[19] It was also, for many, the only avenue to a life of professional service to the community at large. In the age before the Peace Corps, VISTA, and ACTION, to live single in a life of service was not considered a respectable option, so the only fertile ground for the seed of such dedication was membership in the priesthood or a religious order. In this way the stigma and pressure commonly associated with bachelorhood or spinsterhood was transformed into respect for a vowed life as a priest, brother, or sister.[20] The anxieties of parents and friends about "settling down" would subside when a young man or woman's call to service took the form of a vocation rather than apparent eccentricity, particularly in an age when sexist stereotypes of "masculine" and "feminine" adult roles were not questioned as they have been of late.[21]

By the time of Vatican II, vocations to religious orders and to the priesthood seemed to be reaching a peak. But there was developing in the Catholic community a whole new series of relationships between lay and clerical or "religious" roles in the Church.

One factor was the "lay apostolate" movement, which received substantial support from modern popes such as Pius XII. The basic thesis was that the cleric belonged in the sanctuary and the pulpit, and the lay Catholic in the marketplace. According to this line of thinking (evident in the "social encyclicals" of the twentieth century and even the late nineteenth century),[22] the involvement of nuns, brothers, and priests in social, political, or economic questions with moral implications was necessary only insofar as it was required to alert and catalyze the laity,

---

[19] See Andrew M. Greeley, *From Backwater to Mainstream: A Profile of Catholic Higher Education.* First of a Series of Profiles sponsored by the Carnegie Commission on Higher Education (New York: McGraw-Hill, 1969). See also my article, "Permanent Deacons: A Lesser Caste?" *Commonweal,* Vol. 97, No. 14 (January 12, 1973).

[20] I am here using the terms as they commonly apply to members of religious orders of men and women.

[21] See George Devine, *Transformation in Christ* (Staten Island, N.Y.: Alba House, 1972), chap. 7.

[22] See Charles E. Curran, "Roman Catholic Social Ethics: Past, Present and Future," in *That They May Live: Theological Reflections on the Quality of Life,* ed. George Devine (Staten Island, N.Y.: Alba House, 1972), pp. 87–122.

who could then "take over" by discerning and implementing the moral imperatives of the Church in specific situations. Thus there was much enthusiasm in the Church for lay Catholic involvement in unions, fields like sociology and economics, and the sort of "new politics" that were heralded by Eugene McCarthy and the Kennedy Brothers.

Taken a step further, the "lay apostolate" line of thought argued for increased lay Catholic involvement in apostolic endeavors [23] previously thought to be clerical or religious-order domain. It became fashionable to advocate increased lay involvement in the direction of various Catholic activities, far beyond fund drives and Holy Name Society parades. Laymen were becoming editors of diocesan newspapers, accepted members of Catholic school faculties, and even professors of philosophy in Catholic colleges. The next step was the professional involvement of the Catholic lay person in the study and teaching of theology itself.

The sort of view described here, combined with a modicum of healthy reaction against the ubiquitous clerical and "religious" influence of the recent past, resulted, at least for a time, in a minimalistic attitude with respect to the role of the priest, nun, or religious brother in the Catholic community. During this phase a number of the more extreme lay activists seemed to feel that a member of a religious order should perform no function in the Church save that of communal prayer, since that alone appeared essential to membership in a religious community, or that a priest should perform no function not directly connected to his ordination (celebration of Mass and administration of some other sacraments, etc.). This type of viewpoint, with its implication that virtually all leadership in the Catholic community should be taken over by the laity with great haste, was unrealistic in its assessments of clergy and religious-order members. Many a vocation to priestly or religious life had ridden on the coattails of a vocation for work that at the time could only have been effectively performed by priests or members of religious orders: teaching or doing administrative tasks in Catholic schools; working in Catholic hospitals; writing for the Catholic press, etc. A good number of priests, brothers, and sisters had actually had "hyphenated vocations" as nurse-sister, professor-brother, musician-priest, and others. To suddenly question their dual vocations was to question the very persons who had opted for the vocations in the first place. Not only that, but this assessment of the laity unrealistically assumed that the prototypical American Catholic layman was a member of the *cognoscenti* who had read every-one from St. Paul to Pope Pius XII on the Mystical Body,[24] Cardinals

---

23 Apostolic meaning those things that carry out the function of "apostles," not in the limited sense of Peter and the Twelve, but literally from the Greek *apostolos* (messenger), i.e., any work of spreading or implementing the Gospel message of Jesus.

24 1 Cor. 12:4–31, Eph. 4:1–5:20, and AAS XXXV (1943), 193–248.

Newman and Suhard on the layman in the Church, and lay authors like Donald J. Thorman [25] (who wrote *The Emerging Layman*). This type of attitude, while quite fashionable for its de-emphasis of the clergy (a sort of *a*-clericalism, as opposed to *anti*-clericalism), suggested that every layman was infinitely competent and almost every priest, brother, or nun was a usurper.

The attitudes of some of the laity and the reactions of some clerics and religious can be illustrated by recounting an experience from my theological studies at Marquette, during the transitional phase of the Second Vatican Council in 1963. At that time it was the fashion for the graduate theology students to gather in someone's apartment on Friday evenings for beer and pizza (cheese pizza, since abstinence from meat still obtained on Fridays). Approximately half of the students were lay men and women, another forty percent were nuns, and about ten percent were priests sent by their orders or dioceses for further academic study in theology, in preparation for the same college professorships and other positions the lay students and nuns were preparing for. The *soirée* was always lay-dominated both in number and in tone, and the party talk usually gravitated toward the coming of age of the Catholic layman and the passing of a priest-dominated American Catholic experience. Most of the enthusiasts were in their early twenties, and any mention of established clerical figures in the American Church save liberal heroes like Bishop John Wright tended to be humorously patronizing. As the gathering was ending, one of the lay women in the group turned to a departing Jesuit student and asked, "Father, before you go, will you give us your blessing?" He replied, "I'd be glad to, Mary. It's the first time in weeks anyone's implied that I can do anything but say Mass and hear confessions!"

Given this sort of climate, it is not hard to see how the "lay apostolate" movement seemed to ebb in the wake of Vatican II,[26] and many clerics and religious-order members on the American Catholic scene preferred to decline the lay activists' invitation to step aside. In more conservative pockets of Catholic America, there had been incidents of clerical backlash by the early sixties, such as the replacement of lay editor John O'Connor by a monsignor at *The Monitor* in San Francisco.[27] Now, in the later years of the "decade of disillusionment," the examples

---

[25] Donald J. Thorman, *The Emerging Layman* (Garden City, N.Y.: Doubleday & Co., Inc., 1962).

[26] Devine, "Deacons," *Commonweal, Time*, Vol. 101, No. 6 (February 5, 1973), 64f.

[27] O'Connor was demoted to Associate Editor, with Msgr. Francis Quinn taking over as editor. Archbishop McGucken reportedly considered O'Connor "imprudent" and wanted a priest as editor. O'Connor subsequently left.

came more quickly, in greater numbers, and in more diverse spheres of Catholic life, owing either to clericalism, an unhappy maiden voyage with a new lay crew, or both. In many Catholic colleges, the layman was asked out of the theological forum almost as quickly as he had been invited in.[28] In many parishes, lay directors of religious education were hired after recruitment periods of up to a year, and fired in less than half that time on the job.[29] In a variety of Catholic institutions, fault was found with lay administrators who were highly certified but who seemed unable to fathom the intangible essentials of their institution's identity.[30] In less tense times, each instance might have been judged solely on its own merits, but in this period of anxious transition and reaction, each instance was in danger of becoming unwittingly a test case or *cause célèbre,* apt to wind up in the pages of *The National Catholic Reporter.*

Not only could each case become a battle, but it was also difficult to discern just where the battlefield was. For some, it was clearly and simply a matter of personnel management and efficient utilization of resources. In this context, one could argue for the freeing of priests from "non-priestly" obligations so that they could more effectively dispense the sacraments. On the other hand, the same frame of reference could argue for minimization of lay personnel, since they were more costly and less docile. For still others, though, the tension was theological, with respect to the priest or religious-order member as one among a special caste.[31] The New Testament had identified all members of Christ's Church as "a holy nation, a royal priesthood," [32] sharers in Jesus' function of mediating between mankind and God the Father.[33] But within that context, Catholics (and most other Christians) recognized a specifically *ordained* priesthood, along with other special ranks of ministry, bishop

---

28 See my articles on the layman in Roman Catholic theology in the 1960s and early 1970s in *U.S. Catholic* (with R.J. Byrne) 30:55–6, March, 1965; *U.S. Catholic and Jubilee* 34:39–42, March, 1969; and *The New York Times,* October 31, 1971, Sec. 4, "The Week in Review," p. 14.

29 Ibid. Also see Art Winter, "The Lay Theologian Tragedy," *The National Catholic Reporter,* July 23, 1969, and Devine, "Deacons," *Commonweal.*

30 Interestingly enough, many Catholic institutions, e.g., colleges, which dropped statutes or traditions requiring clerical or religious administrators, found themselves choosing clerics or religious over lay candidates under pressure from the *lay* constituency of the institution in question, who felt the identity and traditions of the institution in question could be understood and preserved better by a religious or cleric, and who obviously were not about to share the minority opinion of the "lay activists." Indeed, in many such instances, the lay constituency of the institution was far more "conservative" than the clergy and religious themselves.

31 Though I disagree with his basic theses and conclusions, Michael F. Valente advances some interesting arguments on this particular question in his book *Sex: The Radical View of a Catholic Theologian* (Milwaukee: Bruce, 1970).

32 I Pet. 2:9.

33 See AAS XXXV (1943): 193–248.

and deacon.[34] These were admitted to their roles by the authority of the Church in a solemn manner meant to last a lifetime.[35] The strength and spirituality required for them to perform their sacramental functions and services in the Church were not only vital to these sacramental ends; they were, moreover, elements that went to make up a priestly [36] *state of life.*

This state of life involved a particular approach to prayer: not only ministerial involvement in the Mass, but also daily recitation of the monastic prayer radiating from the Eucharist, the Divine Office.[37] This obligation of the ordained was also extended to nuns and brothers in religious vows, although some orders used a "Little Office" that was shorter. A special type of garb was normally mandated for priests, as for religious brothers and sisters.[38] Not only the monastic orders, but even the "secular" diocesan priesthood [39] showed the influence of monasticism [40] which involved special places for community residence (cloistered, officially or otherwise),[41] restrictions concerning the recreations one chose and the company one kept,[42] and even strict supervision over what one read or wrote.[43] The strictures placed upon priests and re-

---

[34] Since the permanent diaconate (those deacons not preparing for priesthood) fell into disuse for centuries before the present era, and the rank of bishop is classically understood as the fulfillment or epitome of priesthood, we will be using here the generic terms relating to priesthood.

[35] However, priests or deacons can be released from the privileges and obligations of their states for grave reason. The number of cases in which this has taken place has been hard to calculate until recently, since secrecy was commonly imposed as a condition of such a release or "laicization."

[36] See fn. 34.

[37] The Divine Office, according to *The Maryknoll Catholic Dictionary*, pp. 185–86, is "a work done for God ... the public liturgical prayer of the Church distinct from the ... sacramental liturgies. Its purpose is the sanctification of the day through formal prayer at stated hours."

[38] I.e., the clerical black suit and Roman collar, or the religious "habit." Some groups have no official "habit," like the Jesuits, whose garb imitates that of the "secular" clergy in the region.

[39] So called because not officially monastic, although monastic views and styles have long typified both "religious" and "secular" priests.

[40] Not limited in this sense to medieval Western monasticism, since some operative elements of Byzantine monasticism are present as well.

[41] Commonly believed to be limited to members of the order; canonically "off limits" to members of the opposite sex. "Cloister" usually pertains to the living quarters, and often recreational and eating facilities in the residences of religious orders.

[42] Religious orders often counselled against the cultivation of "particular friendships," the reading of too much "secular" literature, etc.

[43] In some seminaries and religious houses, secular newspapers, etc., were forbidden. It has long been the practice, moreover, for seminarians, priests, and religious to submit for approval to their superiors in their orders or dioceses any material for possible publication (independently of and prior to the question of *Imprimatur*). Many seminaries, convents, and abbeys until recently censored incoming and outgoing mail.

ligious brothers and sisters were more than adequate for their functions in community service. But they signified more than mere support for professional dispatch of duties; they were part of a special identity of the holy man or woman in the Church of Christ.

Much has been made in Roman Catholic liturgy of the "canonical" digits, that is, those fingers which priests use to handle the Sacred Host after the Consecration of the Mass, specifically designated and revered for this sacramental act.[44] By way of extension, the entire body and spirit of the man or woman committed to priesthood or religious vows was seen as specially consecrated or dedicated to God, and this was manifested in the commitment of body and soul to celibacy,[45] prayer,[46] and witness to the coming of a kingdom not of this world.[47] In every expression, every gesture, every movement, in details of life large and minute,[48] the ordained priest or the vowed brother or sister was the epitome of a Catholic identity "in the world, but not of it."[49] Although all Catholics were expected to adhere to their obligations as mediators between the Trinity and the world, as sharers in the one true priesthood of Jesus, only those so named by Holy Orders would properly be acknowledged as priests. So, too, were all Catholics expected to adhere to their religious faith, yet only those who had taken formal vows of poverty, chastity, and obedience [50] were called "in religion" or "religious." [51]

---

[44] See Garry Wills, *Bare Ruined Choirs: Doubt, Prophecy and Radical Religion* (Garden City, N.Y.: Doubleday & Co., Inc., 1972), p. 65.

[45] Abstinence from marriage and activities which might lead to it, e.g., courtship. Celibacy is not to be confused with virginity (e.g., a widow or widower could take a vow of celibacy, as could someone who had committed and repented of illicit sexual intercourse). Celibacy is often spoken of as coextensive with a religious vow of chastity. The difference between the two is that celibacy is not a vow in the classic sense, but a canonical obligation of priests in the Western rites since the twelfth century, whereas a vow of chastity, like one of poverty or obedience, belongs to membership in a particular order, independent of ordination (i.e., would apply to nuns, or brothers as well as to priests). The fact that it is hard to distinguish between the two shows how monasticism has made its mark on the "secular" priesthood in the Western Church. See fn. 39.

[46] E.g., the Divine Office, etc.

[47] John 18:36.

[48] Postures, ways of walking, etc., were often taught in seminaries, monasteries, and convents under the heading "religious decorum."

[49] John 18:36.

[50] The reader will remember the distinction, however slight, between chastity and celibacy as mentioned in fn. 45. Poverty is a vow of dependence on the religious community, as opposed to one's own self, for material needs, and obedience to religious superiors is likewise a vow in the formal sense, although obedience to authority pertains to "secular" clergy as well, with respect to their bishops.

[51] A nun or brother, a religious-order priest and sometimes even a "secular" priest is frequently spoken of as "a religious" or "in religion." While this custom is on the wane, many orders' members change their names upon reception into the community, having new names "in religion."

The obvious result was a Catholic caste system, with a pyramidal structure with the Pope ranking first, then the cardinals, followed by archbishops, bishops, such ecclesiastical dignitaries as vicars general and protonotaries apostolic, and in turn right and very reverend monsignori, pastors and curates, superiors in religious communities, the members of the communities themselves, seminarians and novices, and finally "the faithful." And membership among those who were simply "the faithful" implied an identity that was almost negative. As millions of Catholics had learned in their *Baltimore Catechisms*: the laity are those members of the Church who are neither priests nor "religious." [52]

The Second Vatican Council sought to change that. Drawing upon the rich sources of scripture and Church tradition, the decrees of the Council spoke not of a pyramid, but of the People of God.[53] Though there would be no diminution of authority as exercised by Pope, bishop, or pastor, it was clear that this was authority in the sense of service to the community, whose beneficent exercise was understood in terms of the good of the whole.[54] Briefly, authority should not be confused with autocracy. And Christians whose task it was to exercise authority should not have envisioned this role as anything but a rather difficult position for the sake of the Church. Indeed, Christian authorities were markedly different from other authority figures in "the world," since authorities in the Church were the servants and not the served. This view of authority was hardly new to the Church, but it was being stated anew at a time when the Church was undergoing an official period of self-reevaluation in the Conciliar forum. Moreover, the documents of Vatican II spelled out some of the implications of this view. One of these was the notion of authority as "collegial" or shared. The prime model of this was the "college" or assembly of the Apostles immediately after Jesus' earthly ministry, when the primacy of the Rock (Peter) was balanced by his accountability to the entire group.[55] Church history after the apostolic era continued to supply examples of authority exercised "at the top" in consultation either with the Church as a whole, or with representatives

---

[52] Michael A. McGuire, ed., *Baltimore Catechism No. 2* (New York: Benziger Brothers, Inc., 1962), New Revised Edition, pp. 65, 67.

[53] This notion, deeply rooted in the Scriptures, occurs frequently in Vatican II decrees, especially the Dogmatic Constitution on the Church (*Lumen gentium*). See Walter M. Abbott, ed., *The Documents of Vatican II* (New York: America Press/Association Press/Guild Press, 1966).

[54] This can be seen from a literal understanding of the Latin *auctor* (one who gives or fosters life), thus *auctoritas* as a function of giving or fostering life within the community.

[55] The chief example of this is the Council of Jerusalem, the gathering of the Apostolic college to decide how to deal with the question of the Juda-izers. Acts 15.

of the whole Church. This took the form of a series of councils,[56] referral of certain situations for treatment to local authorities out of regard for their competence,[57] and Pope Pius XII's investigation of widespread Catholic faith and practice before formally defining the dogma of the Assumption of the Blessed Virgin in 1950.[58]

In the 1960s, it was feared that Catholics' view of authority in the Church had developed a sort of astigmatism that militated against a balanced view. The decrees of Vatican II did not alter the reality of Church authority, but hoped to provide a corrective lens that would enable the Catholic community to see aright the balance between authoritative power and the authority that necessarily resides in the Church as a whole. Practically speaking, this meant an ongoing series of synods (meetings of bishops) after the formal conclusion of the Council at Rome. Locally, it meant national conferences of bishops representing the Church in different regions. Closer to home, it meant pastoral councils on diocesan and even parish levels, with elections of parishioners to serve as representatives of their fellows. (In the United States, this took on the trappings of campaigns, speeches, promotional literature, and so on, much in keeping with the national political experience.)

If there had been a balanced view of the Church's authority, such announcements from Rome would hardly have caused a stir. But in a Church where authority had become too top-heavy and the laity—apart from the vanguard who attended colleges or read progressive authors— too passive, the experience would be awkward. In one parish the monsignor would lament, "Now they're going to let some housewife tell me how to run my parish!" While such would hardly be the case, pastor after pastor would seek to engineer a parish council election that he might use as a smoke screen or rubber stamp in case the going got tough. In many another instance, the laity—mostly *not* readers of people like Thorman or veterans of groups like the Vernacular Society or the Christian Family Movement—were ill at ease when a new mode of activity came to be expected of them. In one large diocese, the Archbishop (in regular priestly attire, without the embellishments of his

---

[56] For a listing of the Councils of the Church, excepting Vatican II which took place after this publication, see a compilation of Church documents edited at the Jesuits' theologate in Kansas under the title *The Church Teaches* (Milwaukee: Bruce, 1955), p. 368f.

[57] DS 225–26. In the instance of Pelagius, the North African bishops meeting at Carthage were considered the competent authority by the Pope, who referred the matter to them for study and upheld their judgment. This is, of course, but one example. See *The Church Teaches*, No. 527f.

[58] DS 2803–4. Pius XII reportedly circularized bishops, inquiring about the belief and worship of Catholics around the world before declaring formally that Catholics believed the Virgin to have been assumed into heaven.

office) sat on a folding chair on a basketball court, surrounded by lay diocesan-council representatives, and asked for their suggestions and criticisms, and their silent awe was as genuine as his explicit request.

However, the sort of thing we have spoken of here remains in the realm of logistics and management, rather than theological disputes. The theological disputation came, though, invited or not. It came as part of the new world view considered in the first chapter, a fresh way of looking at Christian faith in the world and at what constituted holiness. If holiness were no longer to be seen as restricted to the sanctuary, or the sacred objects of the liturgy, or a particular way of life lived carefully among one's own kind, then it might even follow that holiness or religiousness would no longer seem restricted to "religious" or priestly life in the formal sense. An active life of holiness in the Christian apostolate could perhaps be exercised by the married lay Catholic executive in suburbia (who perhaps, but not necessarily, belonged to his parish council) just as well as by the vowed religious-order member in a monastery or convent. Poverty of spirit could be exercised by a father or mother in a family just as validly as by a sister or brother in an order. Chastity—the rightful exercise of one's sexuality in all its dimensions—could be observed just as meaningfully by the married as by the professedly celibate.[59] Obedience to the will of God as taught by legitimate authority would obtain for all believers, even though the forms of authority they obeyed might differ. The "religious," in short, had no monopoly on religion, and many of their distinguishing trappings began to fall by the wayside, often dropped by self-conscious "religious" themselves.

The "religious," being among the first to receive the latest bulletins of contemporary theological insight, would often be the first to call for their practical implementation. Lines of demarcation were disappearing. Priests were less quick to move toward this new informality, but nuns and brothers now began asking their lay fellows to address them by first names without the ubiquitous preface "Brother" or "Sister" (often "Str" in American Catholic patois). Going even further, order after order not only discontinued the practice of taking a new name upon reception, but even effected a rollback, allowing members to revert to their original names. So Basilides became Andy, and Trinitas became Eleanor, and Mary Edward became Ginny, and Camillus became Don, and Mother Dorothea became Pat. Clothing, of course, began to correspond to the new way of things. The habits, guimpes, cowls, scapulars, and wimples, many "religious" felt, were simply another unnecessary separation between "religious" and their fellows. In some communities, religious garb

---

[59] For an explanation of chastity and celibacy and the distinctions between them, see chapter 1, fn. 9 and chapter 2, fn. 45.

became modified or simplified. In others it was done away with altogether (or at least no longer required, leaving only a few electing it). The collar associated with some orders of brothers gave way to the tie (*not* black) or the turtleneck. The religious dress of females came to be replaced by skirts and sweaters.

For priests, distinguished not only by lifestyle from the laity but also by Holy Orders, the change did not take effect as rapidly or in as widespread a fashion. Indeed, the bulk of American priests deplored the changes around them as garish and tasteless (as they sometimes were) or ignored them as needless and silly (as they also occasionally were). But one could often find a priest, engaged in some priestly or professional pursuit away from the eye of his pastor or bishop, trying out the new styles he had learned from the members of religious orders. Theological conventions and the summer sessions of Catholic universities began to attract a host of rainbow-clad clerics who were more immediately recognizable in mufti than they would ever have been in conventional priestly attire.

One must not get the impression that this was simply a revolution in style. It was a shedding and even renunciation of a whole set of rigors and rituals of which the purpose had been to reinforce a distinctly separate and special way of life and identity for the Catholic cleric and "religious." In not a few cases, taking away some of these elements meant more than just simplifying the exterior; it meant weakening some of the interior supports. Many religious-order members or clerics, who all through adolescent and adult life had learned a lifestyle different from (and "superior to") the average lay Catholic, began to ask themselves: *Who am I? Is it all worth it?* Some who had developed strong identities and insights would answer the first of those questions boldly and the second affirmatively, with hardly a second thought. Some others would come to the same conclusions eventually, but only after some agonizing. Still others would find that they had been able to accept their lives as priests or religious only in "package deals," and that the elimination of these seemingly trivial details was like yanking the center can from a display of canned goods; their fragile commitments shattered easily, and in all too many cases, so did their psyches. Yet another group was able to see the priesthood or the vowed religious life as worthwhile indeed, but not for themselves: they sought exclaustration,[60] dispensation,[61] laiciza-

---

[60] Exclaustration means permission to leave one's religious order; it is often granted on an interim basis for a year, then can be granted finally. Before exclaustration is final, one can live a life similar to that of an ordinary lay person in most ways, but is not free to marry, owing to the obligations involved in a vow of chastity.

[61] Dispensation means dispensation from a canonical obligation of celibacy for a priest, or from a religious vow of poverty, chastity, or obedience (the three are taken together and dispensed from together) in the case of a religious-order member.

tion,[62] and searched for new lives—in many cases trying to go back to the fork in the road and take the directions they had originally forsaken.

For some, this meant acting out of a Catholic religious commitment, as a lay teacher in a Catholic school, as a lay worker in a Catholic hospital or orphanage, or as a lay writer for the Catholic press.[63] For some others, it meant acting out such a commitment in secular organizations that had been legitimized by the theological and political movements of the early 1960s: urban work, VISTA, the Peace Corps, teaching the retarded or disadvantaged in public schools (a former nemesis), and the like.

The impact of this reexamination of priestly and religious life upon the American Church was not easily absorbed. Some of those who opted out of their previous commitments and lifestyles were among the more prominent leaders of American Catholics, especially in progressive circles, like Jacqueline Grennan and Maryellen Muckenhirn, who left their convents, and James Shannon, who even gave up an auxiliary bishopric. Some were those "pillars" whom lay and "religious" Catholics alike had counted on to stick with it and provide leadership for the rest no matter how tough it got, and whose announcements of departure (Father DeLeers in Wisconsin and Monsignor Murray in San Francisco, for example) caused many to feel bewildered, if not betrayed. There were also those whose very images had lent credibility to reform movements within the American Church, especially within religious orders, and whose leave-taking threatened to undo much of the work they had already achieved (like Bernard Cooke).

Among the participants in the "exodus" were the authors of wide-selling books, who left the Church outright. But the scandal of these people was rationalized: after all, James Kavanaugh was emotionally disturbed, and Gabriel Longo was immature, dishonest, and spiteful.[64] When news came from England that Charles Davis was quitting, this was easily categorized as complex intellectual agony. But what of those who appeared to love the Church enough to leave that particular way of life within the Church but not the Church itself? Who *announced*, but could not *denounce?* Who even went through the lengthy and sometimes humiliat-

---

[62] Laicization is the "making-a-layman" of someone who has been ordained a priest or deacon. While laicization removes the prerogatives of office, it often allows that some of these may be exercised thereafter in an emergency (e.g., a priest hearing a deathbed confession) and it does not automatically include permission to marry, which involves a separate permission.

[63] See Wills, *Bare Ruined Choirs,* chap. 2.

[64] Gabriel Longo, *Spoiled Priest* (New York: University Books, Inc., 1966); James Kavanaugh, *A Modern Priest Looks at His Outdated Church* (New York: Trident Press, 1967).

ing processes of formal release from religious obligations?[65] Some observers tried to attribute the whole movement to one cause—celibacy. Others were more perceptive and were inclined to ask: if celibacy had not been responsible for mass defections from the ranks of religious orders and the priesthood before this, why should it become so all of a sudden? Yet there seemed to be some sort of relationship between a sudden diminution of clerical and religious ranks, the large number of ex-religious and ex-clergy opting marriage, and the obvious fact that according to Catholic discipline one could not be a priest or a member of a religious order *and* marry.[66]

One perceptive observer, Jesuit sociologist Eugene J. Schallert, articulates a theory of the "crucial other." According to Schallert, a priest (or religious-order member) would be likely to experience a vocational identity crisis in a time of sudden and multifaceted change in Church and world alike, and to seek help, even subconsciously, from another. In some instances, the theory states, religious and priests who fail to find empathy or assistance within their religious structures (or who are not inclined or able to look there) gravitate toward heterosexual friendship which tends to "back into" marriage, often a marriage which is a mistake and which is either torturous, or terminated a short time after it takes place.[67] In Schallert's view, the key element is not celibacy versus marriage, but what sociologists often term "job frustration," and the frustrated priest or religious is likely to marry or not depending on the "crucial other" he encounters in his frustration.

Much the same view is expressed by Andrew Greeley, among others, when he points out that priests forsake the active ministry or become disillusioned with it for myriad reasons other than the regulation of celibacy, especially that will-o'-the-wisp generically described as job frustration.[68] Job frustration is by no means limited to ministers, of course. Executives, salesmen, and teachers all face it in one form or another, but they all have certain safety valves unavailable to the cleric: promotions come far more readily, resignation without disgrace is far more possible, and duties are often more clearly defined in an age of

---

[65] See *Commonweal's* narrative "Trial by Laicization," Vol. 87, No. 10 (December 8, 1967), 328ff.

[66] Priesthood and marriage have been mutually exclusive in the Roman Rite (which includes over 90% of the world's Catholics) since the twelfth century; religious-order membership, of course, includes a vow of chastity, i.e., celibacy.

[67] Eugene J. Schallert and Jacqueline M. Kelley, "Some Factors Associated with Voluntary Withdrawal from the Catholic Priesthood," *Lumen Vitae* XXV, 3 (1970), 425–60.

[68] Andrew M. Greeley, *Priests in the United States: Reflections on a Survey* (Garden City, N.Y.: Doubleday & Co., Inc., 1972). Also see Schallert's review of same in *The National Catholic Reporter*, April 28, 1972, p. 14.

ever more detailed job descriptions. Today's priest (or religious-order member) may find himself assigned to a task in which responsibilities are vague, without adequate support from superiors, or perhaps with even direct opposition from superiors who view too much activity from below as unsettling. Often such a cleric may consider himself (rightly or not) more qualified than those above him, but he knows that his superiors are likely to remain entrenched until he, at the age of fifty or over, is finally able to move into a "middle management" position (around the time many an executive in "the world" begins to plan retirement!).[69]

Some inventive ministers are often able to take just the sort of unhappy circumstances described above and turn them to gain for their apostolic goals, but many are not so resourceful and often wonder aloud if they should be expected to deal with such obstacles as a matter of course. At all events, this type of log jam is considered by many ecclesiastical commentators as more significant than the celibacy rule in the attrition from priestly ranks that has become so newsworthy within recent years.

With this problematic situation in mind, the Church is attempting to make the priesthood (and religious-order life) more viable for actual and prospective members. In most dioceses, priests are represented in pastoral councils and priests' senates. Although there is always a danger that such a group could be a rubber stamp for the hierarchy, or intimidated by it, experience thus far indicates some successful attempts at representation within the ranks of the ministry. Likewise, religious orders are more and more inclined to put important (and even not so important) questions to the forum of a chapter (for example, whether to retain, abolish, or make optional the traditional habit or garb of a particular community). Furthermore, bishops and religious superiors are relying more and more on the expressed wishes of individual priests and brothers and nuns as regards assignment. Some even utilize personnel committees to assess needs and consider requests for assignment in light of them. A cleric under such a system might even have some form of appeal over a disappointing decision concerning assignment or transfer. This is a far cry from the days, even recently, when a superior could assign a member of his order or a bishop could assign a priest without having to define the terms of the assignment or defend its selection.

For some, this is seen as a boon. It now becomes possible in some religious communities for an entering member to have great choice in a professional career (teaching of a particular subject on a specific level, urban work, psychology, etc.) or even in geographical area assignment,

---

[69] For a fictional treatment of the same situation, see Ralph McInerny, *The Priest* (New York: Avon, 1974).

rather than to have these dictated by a religious superior's perception of the demands of the community's apostolic commitments. But even with all these changes, it can hardly be argued that a commitment to priestly or religious-order life is more predictable than it was in ages past. On the contrary, increased freedom brings with it fewer predictable options. For example, the Jesuits, long committed to high schools and colleges in the United States and elsewhere, are attracting a number of young men who subscribe to the spirit of the Society of Jesus, but who feel that their Order's mission today lies outside the classroom and in other fields.[70] A number of young Jesuits have told their superiors that they are not interested in teaching at Fordham or Loyola, and the superiors (no doubt having their own second thoughts about their heavy commitments to expensive universities) are honoring many of those choices. It is reported that the Vincentians (best known for St. John's in New York) are reconsidering their own involvement in university education, and that the Religious of the Sacred Heart of Jesus ("Madams") are now envisioning an apostolate which more explicitly includes the poor, and not just the rich. In one sense, this is an exercise in choice; in another, it can be unsettling to those members of an order who are committed to the traditional apostolate of their community.

No less buffeted by the winds of change will be the diocesan priest, now often called upon to learn Spanish in the seminary in preparation for work in a Hispanic-American parish or assigned to serve a ghetto community whose flock is mostly non-Catholic and suspicious of the "white man's religion." Adaptation to new needs in new times will call for more than the resourcefulness of Odysseus and the patience of Job. There will also be great need for the spiritual maturity and dedication so long associated with clerical life that had been built on rocks of stability and predictability.

Indications like these bring up the whole question of the clergy of the future, both quantitatively and qualitatively. What role will the cleric play in the life of the community in the future, and how will the Church meet its needs?

Contrary to many opinions, there is probably no genuine dearth of clergy in the United States (or, for that matter, in some other countries). However, gone forever are the days when the priest, brother, or nun had to do virtually everything that needed doing in the Catholic community. The clergy and religious orders need no longer be omnipresent, and saturating the community with their ranks. (Indeed, this was possibly unnecessary in the first place.) Today's Catholic in America tends to look

---

[70] See Robert Blair Kaiser, "The Remaking of the Jesuit Colleges," *World* 1:11 (November 21, 1972), 30ff.

less and less to his Church for the fulfillment of needs which are not explicitly religious. More and more, secular agencies are being sought out for aid which is becoming increasingly efficient and economical in such areas as those of health care, education, social needs, and others. Now schools and hospitals operated under Catholic auspices are more often chosen for their general excellence than merely their religious affiliation. The Church, particularly the parochial church at the local level, is no longer the focal point of community activity for Catholics that it had been for so long in so many Catholic ghettos in the United States. No longer does the typical American Catholic life seem to revolve around the Knights of Columbus, the Rosary and Altar Society, the Holy Name Society, the C.Y.O.,[71] or separate Catholic groups of boy and girl scouts.[72] In most dioceses, the official Catholic newspaper receives far lower advertising and subscription revenue than it did even a few years ago.[73] Likewise, many Catholic magazines and periodicals have become superfluous over the past decade, and many more are undergoing the sort of identity crisis ("What really is our purpose?") that may result in their demise.

Part of the phenomenon just described could be attributed to a sort of general malaise among American Catholics since the Vatican Council ended in 1965. Led to believe that things would only improve, American Catholics have come to find many of their traditions challenged and uprooted, and entire ways of life called into question, particularly the religious-order members and clergy.[74] There is less docility toward and less reliance upon the Catholic organizational structure, and Catholics in America, emerging from a ghetto existence which was a way of life apart, feel less need to socialize and commiserate with fellow Catholics exclusively. Breathing the same air as their non-Catholic acquaintances might be a fresh and certainly less painful experience these days. This helps to explain the lessening dependence of American Catholics on Catholic institutions, and thus on "religious" and clerical members who staff those institutions.

Moreover, there is apt to be less reliance upon the religious-order member or the priest as personal religious leader. The conservative Irish-Catholic American who had so exclusively looked to priestly authority

---

[71] Catholic Youth Organization, involved typically in sports and social functions for teenagers and younger children.

[72] Although I know of no such thing officially, there existed in some localities not long ago dens or similar groupings of scouts that were composed totally of parochial school students or Catholics, while dens composed of "non-Catholics" existed in the same areas.

[73] John Deedy, "Nobody here but us editors ...", *Overview* (special report), 1972.

[74] Devine, *Transformation in Christ,* chap. 5.

would not now consider himself a sheep in the flock of Father Berrigan, any more than an Italian-American Catholic is likely to consider a priest named Groppi admirable in his people's history. The priest (or religious-order member) since Vatican II too often seemed to represent people not of his own kind, people who appeared to need the help more. To many American Catholics, representing the type of "middle American" or "silent majority" attitude that prevailed in the presidential elections of 1968 and 1972, this sort of thing is an unforgivable desertion. At the same time, a significant number of younger, more liberally oriented Catholics do not feel they can endorse someone who speaks with the Church's authority but with opinions that they feel do not represent their own positions in particular instances. A case in point would be the disclaimer issued in behalf of a regional group of Catholic laity when Cardinal Krol of Philadelphia spoke out about abortion in 1973:

> Archbishop John Cardinal Krol's remarks attacking last week's Supreme Court decision liberalizing abortion laws do not represent the views of all Pennsylvania Roman Catholics, according to a statement released last Tuesday by the Independent Catholic Laity Association. . . .
>
> Association Secretary Dr. Joseph Skehan said the Archbishop's stand that the ruling permitting abortions into the sixth month of pregnancy is an "unspeakable tragedy," is not shared by some 25,000 Pennsylvania lay Catholics. . . .
>
> "No doubt some share his views . . . . But as public opinion polls show, many Catholic laity do not . . . . Archbishop Krol's statements should not be interpreted as those of the entire Catholic community," Dr. Skehan said.[75]

The clergy, previously considered the spokesmen for Catholics en masse, were now being contradicted or at least challenged every time they spoke too far to the left or right of their constituencies. The Vatican Council had taught lessons about religious freedom and individual conscience, and it appeared that in the wake of the exercise, the lay students were inferring lessons which had possibly not been envisioned.

Moreover, the very ambiance which had set "religious" apart from lay Catholics had been going by the boards, and many lay American Catholics began to feel that their awe of and deference to brothers and sisters had been a nice thing for ages past but might be misplaced in a new era. After all, nuns and religious brothers were able to wear "lay" clothes, able to enter and leave their religious communities and life-styles practically at will, able to carry on in what by former standards

---

[75] *The New York Times,* February 4, 1973.

would have seemed the most outlandish of ways: leaving their humble convents to rent luxury apartments on the East Side of Manhattan; forsaking their teaching commitments to engage in special "experimental" missions; abandoning the white working-class children of the parish to take up placards in favor of the "colored." What sort of respect was this type of "religious" entitled to? Some, surely, but no longer the unquestioning docility of yesteryear.

The American lay Catholic, in an experience not totally unlike that of a child who suddenly becomes orphaned, was being made to grow up in the late 1960s and early 1970s. The experience could not help but be painful for the Church as institution and for each of its individual ministers and members. Through it all, despite all the old trappings and the reassurances that came when the early 1970s attempted to ape the stable 1950s, things would never be the same again, and lay Catholics would rely less and less on the institutional Church and its representatives for their leadership and direction.

None of the above should be interpreted to mean that American Catholics undergoing this series of growing pains would become less religious, for religiousness and dependence on religious authority are not simply interchangeable. Even more than for the "fifties liberal" described with affectionate hindsight by such observers as Wills,[76] it might now be possible for the new American Catholic to be religious without being priest-dominated.

However, the problem in the late 1960s and early 1970s had a way of compounding, and the post-Conciliar malaise translated itself into decreased observance of the more common external signs of religious practice. Thus attendance at Mass, both obligatory and voluntary, dipped noticeably, as did utilization of the Sacrament of Penance (Confession).[77] As the 1970s reached midpoint, there seemed to be no evidence to suggest a sudden swing upward on either front. The same American Catholicism, which in the early 1960s had busily set about building churches and recruiting clergy and religious, would now have reason to think that the churches were too many and too big for worship, and the clergy too numerous.

Despite that, the early 1970s showed a bit of an upswing in some seminary enrollments and in applications to some religious orders. For some, this was a hopeful sign indeed: more laborers for the vineyard of the Lord.[78] But others, like Maryknoll priest-psychologist Eugene C.

---

[76] Wills, *Bare Ruined Choirs,* chaps. 1 and 2.

[77] This will be discussed at much greater length in chapter 5.

[78] John Sprague, "He must increase, I must decrease . . .?" *Overview* (special report), 1973.

Kennedy, viewed the situation less sanguinely, noting that ". . . vocations in some places are increasing, which depresses me." [79] For Kennedy, an upswing in priests' numbers would become a glut for a coming age which would likely no longer be as centered on the community roles of the institutional Church and the ordained clergy. For him a downturn or continued lessening in priestly vocations would be ". . . the solution to the problems we had when the Church was clerically bloated. . . . We need *fewer* priests. . . ." [Emphasis mine.]

Neither Kennedy nor I would suggest that the priesthood will cease to fulfill very special roles within local and even larger communities of American Catholics. The sacramental ministry will doubtless continue to flourish in quality of religious experience and devotion if not in the quantity of its members. This will be so even if the sort of a-clericalism which looks to the priest for little else than sacramental celebration survives. In addition, there will be a good number of American Catholics who will be spiritual, intellectual, and moral leaders, not merely because of, but neither in spite of, their roles as priests, bishops, or religious brothers or sisters, and thus may well take full advantage of their ecclesiastical positions to see and fill the needs of the community for the types of leadership they would offer in any case.

The signs of the times indeed point to fewer priests, nuns, and religious brothers. But those there will understand their roles in ways which are at once more flexible and more substantial, and thus will come to have less expected of them by the community. But each Catholic community must realize the responsibilities and potentialities of all its members if it is to survive as anything but a small and stubborn remnant. To quote Kennedy again: "Only those who long for the restoration of a world that can never be again, would long for seminaries teeming with apple-cheeked youths."

---

[79] *The National Catholic Reporter,* December 15, 1972, p. 6. Kennedy was speaking to a group of deacons, and thus in the context of the restoration of the permanent diaconate in the United States. I admit to rather selective excerption of his remarks so as to demonstrate my agreement with him concerning the necessity for fewer clergy, specifically priests. As to the probable success of the diaconate, Kennedy and I obviously are in disagreement, as can be seen from his article in toto and my own remarks in "Deacons: A Lesser Caste?" *Commonweal* 97:14.

# 3

# Teach Us How to Pray

"Lovely Lady, dressed in blue, teach us how to pray," went the little song the children sang in parochial school,[1] "God was just your little boy, and you know the way!" The song was intended, of course, to foster devotion to both the Blessed Virgin and her divine Son, Jesus. But the route to be taken by this devotion was carefully chosen: to Jesus through Mary. The pious itinerary was indicative of more than simply strong devotion to the Blessed Mother; it was also a sign of a spirituality wherein Catholics considered any of the three Divine Persons in God, including Jesus,[2] well nigh inaccessible without some sort of intermediary. Until about the late 1950s or by early 1960s, many Catholics somehow sensed that to approach God himself too directly would be at least arrogant, if not almost blasphemous. Such an attitude was hardly representative of authentic Catholic tradition, which provides for worship of the Trinity directly as well as for the indirect prayer through Mary and the other Saints; yet such an attitude did have good historical reason to exist.

The primary access route to God for a Catholic was the liturgy of the Mass, in which the Sacrament of the Holy Eucharist is celebrated and

---

[1] The song was used in Catholic elementary schools in the United States until at least the late 1950s. I recall singing it in the 1940s.

[2] The Three Persons in the Blessed Trinity, in Christian dogma and specifically Catholic doctrine, are God the Father, God the Son (Jesus), and God the Holy Spirit (or Holy Ghost).

made available to the Faithful. In antiquity this celebration tended to be intimate, joyous, even somewhat spontaneous. But this did not last long in the history of the Roman Church. As the political unity of the West became increasingly important in the eyes of Church and state alike, Latin continued to be the language of the liturgy long after it had ceased to be the language of the people.[3] Moreover, in A.D. 754, Pepin decreed that Latin rites other than the main one emanating from Rome would have to be suppressed.[4] This meant a uniform liturgy throughout the Western Church,[5] and thus a highly codified ritual recorded in official liturgical books.[6] Since the languages common to the people were not literary languages, i.e., could not be written since they were spoken by illiterates, the Church in the West could not have both a uniform liturgy and a vernacular liturgy. The uniform liturgy in Latin won out, for whatever it turned out to be worth to the unity of the Holy Roman Empire, and its inadequacy for the Church as a total community was not apparent to the churchmen and rulers who were probably as familiar with Latin as they were unfamiliar with the people at large. Attempts to reform the Roman Liturgy in various ways, including its language, might have come into their own around the sixteenth century were it not for the polarized atmosphere that surrounded the Protestant Reformation. The renewal of the liturgy competed with many other concerns on the agenda of the monumental and arduous Council of Trent,[7] and external signs of stability, like the Latin language, were seen as important to preserving the identity and unity of those who remained loyal to the Bishop of Rome.[8] Thus for four centuries more, the liturgy in the Western Church would remain in Latin and would continue to suggest a mysterious division between the sacred mysteries of the altar and the lay congregants in the nave of the church.

------

[3] For more detailed background, see George Devine, *Our Living Liturgy* (Chicago: Claretian Publications, 1966), or *Liturgical Renewal: An Agonizing Reappraisal* (Staten Island, N.Y.: Alba House, 1973), chap. 1.

[4] Ibid.

[5] Devine, *Our Living Liturgy*. In the Eastern Rites, this was not the case, but the Western Church predominated in numbers, as it still does, making the Eastern Rites' experience exceptional. Some of the suppressed Western Rites survived: the Ambrosian Rite in the Archdiocese of Milan, the Mozarabic Rite on one altar of the Cathedral of Toledo in Spain, and the Gallican Rite, in a number of accretions into the Roman Rite which developed after the Roman Rite was ordered for the Frankish region. The monastic rites (Dominican, Praemonstratensian, etc.) have been allowed to survive in their respective communities.

[6] Ibid. The books, such as sacramentary, lectionary, etc., had been combined into the volume *Missale Romanum*. They have since been divided again to reflect the different liturgical roles of celebrant, lector, etc.

[7] Ibid.

[8] Ibid.

The great Jesuit liturgist Josef A. Jungmann has remarked that the Mass, despite such difficulties, remained the chief source of grace for the Church, and that this sacramental efficacy itself suggests the miraculous.[9] Indeed, the piety of the Church continued to revolve around the central celebration of the Eucharist, although many of the lines of communication between layman and altar were indirect and required many supports.

Some of the factors which added to mystification and even obfuscation in the Roman Liturgy were occasioned by theological controversies in Christian history. It is often suggested, for example, that the changing of the altar from a central banquet table to a sort of throne against the back sanctuary wall [10] was a reaction against heresies which compromised the dogma of Jesus' divinity.[11] However, the relationship between faith and worship often worked in the opposite direction, wherein popular preachers introduced into the piety of the Catholic community many notions enjoying no theological basis as such, but which borrowed from liturgical circumstance.[12] Not the least of these was the Latin language itself, little more than a historical accident, which for many Catholics came to be known as insurance for the Church's dogmas, protection against theological confusion and inconsistency, a sign of unity the world over, and a pledge of eternal fidelity between a loving God who offers friendship and pious man who accepts. When these rhapsodies to the Latin liturgy were played and embellished, their composers and performers were often ignorant of such historical facts as the introduction of Latin over Greek as the result of a vernacularist movement between the second and fourth centuries, since the history of the liturgy was not generally well known until quite recently. So it was that with the best of motives, exponents of the Catholic faith attempted to foster the devotion of their fellows by seizing upon even the most incidental of rituals and explaining with seeming verisimilitude their divine origins and meanings. Even when allowances were made for the exotic (the Eastern Rite Catholics, for example, not only had vernacular liturgy but even had married priests who wore beards!), Western Catholics were convinced that they had no alternative to continuing the celebration of the liturgy as they had come to know it; and the bishops, the clergy, and the teachers in Catholic institutions of learning (even on the college level) generally

9 Josef A. Jungmann, *The Mass of the Roman Rite* (New York: Benziger Brothers, Inc., 1959), *Missarum Sollemnia*, one-volume edition, rev. C. Reipe, tr. R. Brunner, p. 55.

10 The recent "altar facing the people" is actually a restoration of a traditional practice, despite many contrary claims by detractors of the practice.

11 See Devine, *Our Living Liturgy*, and Jungmann, *Mass of the Roman Rite*. Christological heresies, i.e., errors concerning the relationship between divinity and humanity in Jesus, are characteristically an overemphasis on one of these aspects at the expense of the other.

12 See Jungmann's description of Amalar in *Mass of the Roman Rite*, p. 66

reinforced the conviction, until as recently as the very eve of the Second Vatican Council.

This meant that the typical Catholic lay person was generally satisfied to attend Mass whenever obliged to, if not more often,[13] without being concerned about the intelligibility of the ritual. What mattered was not intelligibility but sacramental efficacy. What was important was that the celebrant properly enunciated the words of consecration in a way that would be heard by God, whether or not he was heard or understood by man. During the early twentieth century, some of the more educated lay Catholics became interested in owning and using newly available hand missals, small editions of the *Missale Romanum* the priest used at the altar, with the Latin text of the liturgy alternating with the vernacular translation on facing pages.[14] However, for most, keeping up with the rapid pace of the priest's prayers or keeping track of the ribbon markers for the changeable parts of the Mass propers [15] often proved too tedious a chore, and this most direct of indirect accesses to the sanctuary, the missal, tended to retain its original beauty and not to become worn through overuse. Many lay Catholics opted for even less direct means of "praying the Mass." For some it was the Rosary, for others a prayerbook (distinct from the missal in that it was a generic prayerbook, not just a book of liturgical texts), for others a series of favorite personal prayers known by heart, and for still others a practice as old as the venerable churches of Europe: meditation on the mysteries of the faith and their implications, aided by the church architecture, statuary, stained glass, and other liturgical arts, including sacred music.[16] More often than not, the Mass became a vehicle for such indirect routes to God as the veneration of the Virgin or of a particular Saint (e.g., Anthony, Ignatius of Loyola, Francis, Agnes, Anne, Joseph—patron Saint of the Church and of a happy death— or Jude—patron Saint of "lost causes"), often signified by praying before a statue of the particular Saint, or even by the lighting of a vigil light before the statue (a sign of one's continuing prayer, even after one had left the church building itself, asking the Saint's intercession before God).

Early in the twentieth century, Pope Pius X (himself later canonized as patron saint of the Holy Eucharist) called for a renewal in Eucharistic

---

[13] Daily Mass attendance, including Holy Communion, came to be an important element during the liturgical renewal of the early twentieth century, owing to the efforts of Popes Pius X, Pius XI, and Pius XII.

[14] Devine, *Liturgical Renewal*, chap. 2.

[15] Those parts of the Mass proper to the particular feast or seasonal celebration (or special celebration, as in a votive Mass) of the day, i.e., Introit, Collect, etc.

[16] Devine, *Liturgical Renewal*, chaps. 2 and 5.

piety, including frequent reception of Communion and greater intelligibility in the liturgy (beginning with liturgical music, wherein he called for a rediscovery of the beautiful and uncluttered Gregorian Chant).[17] In their turns, Popes Pius XI and Pius XII stressed the same themes, and Catholics would sometimes find themselves asked to join in such practices as "dialogue Mass" (saying the Latin responses as a group in alternation with the prayers of the priest, whereas the congregation's part had previously been recited by the acolyte(s) alone).[18] But such innovations were uncomfortable for most, who would prefer instead to go back in peace to their private devotions, rather than be jarred by the recitation in lock step of a series of phonetically printed foreign phrases like *Ahd dáy-ooom kwee lay-tée-fee-cat yóo-ven-tóo-tem máy-oom.*[19] In many parishes, the dialogue Mass movement disappeared almost as mysteriously as it had appeared, and in many more, it was never even begun.[20] For all practical purposes, then, the "liturgical movement" was relatively unknown to the average American Catholic when the 1960s began. The jolting changes that have since taken place in the liturgy of the Church, particularly in the United States, are by now a matter of record.[21]

The changes in the Roman Catholic liturgy were not supposed to have been a jolt for anyone: they were supposed to have been a smooth transition into a new liturgical piety in the Church which would have been truer to authentic Catholic tradition. The trouble was that though the liturgical experts themselves and even some of the bishops who accepted their recommendations may have understood that, it is now rather sadly clear that most Catholics, including some clergy and even hierarchy, did not. Although the Decree on the Sacred Liturgy from the Second Vatican Council called for careful preparation of the clergy and the laity in advance of the liturgical renovations,[22] this rarely took place on the diocesan or parochial level. What *did* take place, characteristically, was a minimum of instruction in the mechanics of the change (how to say the responses, what hymns would be sung, etc.) without adequate psychological preparation for the fact that the Church

---

17 Ibid.

18 Ibid., chap. 2.

19 *Ad Deum, qui laetificat juventutem meum* (To God, who gives joy to my youth), from the Entrance Rite of the Roman Liturgy.

20 Devine, *Our Living Liturgy.*

21 Ibid., and Devine, *Transformation in Christ* (Staten Island, N.Y.: Alba House, 1972), chaps. 1, 2, 5, and 8.

22 See Walter M. Abbott, ed., *The Documents of Vatican II,* tr. Joseph Gallagher (New York: America Press/Association Press/Guild Press, 1966), paper edition, p. 144.

was suddenly going to change something which it had told people, for years, was not about to be changed. Furthermore, the "something" being changed was not a mere incidental in the hearts of the people (even though it was incidental to the dogma of the Church). It was a way of relating symbolically, of acting out in ritual a deep and complex faith-relationship that could not be understood abstractly nearly so well as it could be ritualized concretely.

In the new order of things, Catholics around the world, and particularly in the United States, found themselves being asked to live out their worshipping lives in a way which may well have been (and which I personally believe is) far more meaningful than what had gone immediately before, but which was in many ways even more foreign to them than the old ways were supposed to have been.

When the mystification was taken out of the Roman liturgy,[23] many Catholics mistakenly believed that the mystery was gone as well. This was hardly the case, in that the mysteries of the Faith were to be made *more* meaningfully intelligible by the liturgical renewal. But when the medium of the Latin language, the *sotto voce* prayers, the priest with his back to the people (standing before them as their representative, facing God, as it were), the beautiful and "Churchy-sounding" foreign phrases in speech and song, the incense (all but eliminated in the new rites), the Rosary (not to be said during Mass), and all the rest were taken away, many Catholics found themselves in a situation not unlike that of one required to stare at the sun with the naked eye. Christ was present in the liturgy of the Word and the Eucharist, there to be met head on, without the layers of intermediaries, in a fashion which would strike the average worshipper as too cerebral and abstract and not tangible enough to get a good grasp on.

Commentators like Garry Wills [24] and James Hitchcock,[25] among others, have noted the Church's mistake in taking away a set of symbolic ways of relating to the Mass without installing another set that would be equally serviceable, or taking care to preserve as many elements from the old set as could be kept.

The mistake appears to have arisen from the wide gulf between the Catholic community as a whole (again including the bulk of the clergy) and the small group of *illuminati* who were tuned into the liturgical movement and the theology and history of the liturgy. These scholars were able to understand the changing of a practice on the grounds that it was an historical accretion, or liturgically improper,

---

[23] C.J. McNaspy, *America* CIX, No. 6 (August 10, 1963).

[24] *Bare Ruined Choirs: Doubt, Prophecy and Radical Religion* (Garden City, N.Y.: Doubleday & Co., 1972).

[25] *The Decline and Fall of Radical Catholicism* (Garden City, N.Y.: Doubleday & Co., 1971).

or simply not as theologically meaningful as that which was about to replace it. They had been influenced by the sort of theological and historical research that had come out of the European monasteries and had begun filtering through a few of the better Catholic seminaries and colleges in America.[26] They were also familiar with and able to fathom such subtleties as the relationship between the daily celebration of Mass and the communal chanting of the Divine Office,[27] or the reasons why the baptismal font should be repositioned to express its relationship to the Sacrament of the Eucharist,[28] or the particular appropriateness of conically-shaped chasubles instead of the old Roman "fiddlebacks." [29] These "liturgical movers" were isolated from the rest of the Catholic community, partly by circumstance. Many of them, for instance, were members of monastic orders and hence ineligible to become bishops or pastors who could influence the Church at the grassroots levels. Some others were lay people whose real influence would show more in the pages of journals like *Worship, Jubilee,* and *Liturgical Arts* than in the total Church community.[30] In addition to their circumstantial isolation, many "liturbugs" (as some derisively called them) were isolated by design, rejected by less sophisticated Catholics (again, many clerics among them) as dilettantes and troublemakers. The result of this sort of isolation was that the liturgically oriented retreated further and further into their own sort of subculture, meeting each other at the same conventions, addressing each other in the same journals, until they became rather out of touch with what the rest of the Church was thinking, feeling, and doing. When the liturgical experts won the day by persuading the bishops to accept their proposed reforms at the Second Vatican Council,[31] they made two gratuitous assumptions. The first was that the Church in general either was learning or would learn enough about the liturgy to appreciate and profit from the renewal,

---

26 Devine, *Liturgical Renewal,* chaps. 2 and 3.

27 A series of prayers corresponding to different times of the day and to the day in the liturgical calendar of the Church, sung communally in monastic orders and said privately by secular clergy. See chapter 2, fn. 37.

28 It was felt for some time that the font should be near the entrance to the church to signify its being the way in which Christians enter the worshipping community. More recently, it has been stressed that Baptism initiates one into the mysteries of the Eucharist, and that the font should therefore be near the altar of eucharistic celebration.

29 The outer vestment, or chasuble, if it is one of the newer ones, appears conelike in shape when laid out flat; the old Roman vestments were called "fiddlebacks" because the back part of the chasuble resembled the shape of a fiddle (the part of the chasuble most often seen by Catholics accustomed to the old practice of Mass facing away from the congregation).

30 Devine, *Liturgical Renewal,* chaps. 2 and 3.

31 Abbott, *Vatican II,* pp. 133–82.

and the second was that the liturgical *periti* [32] would have some hand in executing the reforms of which they had convinced the hierarchy. Instead, the liturgists found themselves condemned to a fate like that of the playwright who is forced to stand in the wings watching his lines butchered by inept actors tutored by a less than enthusiastic director. [33]

The average American Catholic, if he thought about liturgical renewal, thought about it the way the Israelites began to think about Moses when he led them out of Egypt: life under Pharaoh had been no bargain, but the Promised Land had yet to materialize, and life in the desert was becoming increasingly trying. [34]

Several things happened to help the renewal of the liturgy in the American Church. One was the eventual vernacularization of the entire Mass liturgy as it is heard by the people, rather than just the few parts taken out of the Latin by the initial reforms of the Council. [35] Another was the construction of permanent altars facing the people—unlike the temporary altars used in that fashion—which resembled stately tables for the sacrificial banquet of Christ rather than folding tables hastily arranged for a Knights of Columbus meeting. [36] Still another was the gradual acclimation of the people, including new generations of Catholics being educated. [37] One development which has been viewed as a boon and a bane has been the American "folk Mass" movement, which was popular in the late 1960s and included the composition and performance (sometimes with guitar, banjo, or tambourine) of popular religious songs in a folksong or coffee house style, usually combined with a somewhat informal style of liturgical celebration. It was particularly popular among younger members of the worshipping community, but was viewed as approaching blasphemy by some of the more conservative "old line" members of the Church. Also viewed with mixed reactions was the new Order of the Mass or *Ordo Missae* promulgated by Pope Paul to take effect in 1970: this was the finished product, to be used for a time, of the studies and experiments that went on in the half-decade after the initial renovation of the liturgy by Vatican II. The new ritual strove for more flexibility (particularly in the alternate

---

[32] A Latin term meaning experts, used here in a wider sense than simply the official designation of a particular expert as a conciliar *peritus*.

[33] Devine, *Liturgical Renewal*, chaps. 2 and 3.

[34] Devine, *Transformation in Christ*, chaps. 1 and 2.

[35] Abbott, *Vatican II*, pp. 144ff.

[36] It was said that Cardinal McIntyre of Los Angeles would not abide temporary *versus populum* altars, but did not prohibit permanent ones.

[37] The liturgical character of much contemporary religious education is clearly evident, even in the face of criticism from those who would rather see a "return to the Baltimore Catechism."

choices offered for Scriptural readings), simplicity (eliminating many repetitious or overlong aspects of the rite), and even continuity with Christian antiquity (emulating a variety of ancient worship forms). But while its end result might have been a more attractive liturgy, it was simply one more change to a number of Catholics who were already tired of having their prayer lives buffeted by seemingly constant alterations.

In retrospect, it could probably be said with fairness that both liturgical traditionalists, who reacted to changes by establishing centers where the more familiar rites could be continued,[38] and liturgical progressives made the same mistake: they expected too much of the liturgy. This is not to reject the theological truism that the celebration of the liturgy resides at the heart of the Christian life, but it is to point out that even so, some unreasonable expectations were held for the liturgy by its self-styled preservers and adapters alike.

For some "traditionalists" (badly misnamed since they mistook the recent past for authentic tradition),[39] the liturgy became a symbol of historical continuity and of solid and clear identity against Protestantism. Thus it could not change, could not be too simple, and could not be anything less than a repository for all human aspirations in an atmosphere of antique and mystifying splendor. For some "progressives" (badly misnamed since some of their proposals did not ensure progress), the liturgy was envisioned as the almost magical encounter which would transform the gauche into the tasteful, the apathetic into the enthusiastic, and the bigoted into the open-hearted, by virtue of the right translations of the right texts, the right songs, the right vestments, and the right styles in art and architecture. Both of these groups were similar in that both tended to see the value of the liturgy not in terms of its chief role—a celebration of the divine intervention in human history—but rather in terms of its occasional side effects for human aspiration and communal cohesion. By the late 1960s, Catholic writers like Daniel Callahan and others were beginning to wonder about the whole role of the liturgy in the life of the Church.[40]

On a more existential level, many Catholics began to diminish or even cease altogether their participation in the sacramental liturgy. The late 1960s and early 1970s saw survey after survey indicating a

---

38 A prime example of this was the Ave Maria Chapel at Old Westbury, Long Island, operated by Father Gommar DePauw and his Catholic Traditionalist Movement.

39 See Charles Kohli, "A Time to Be at One," in *To Be A Man,* ed. George Devine (Englewood Cliffs, N.J.: Prentice-Hall, Inc., 1969).

40 Daniel Callahan, "Putting the Liturgy in Its Place," *The National Catholic Reporter* 3:40 (August 9, 1967).

decline in attendance at Sunday Mass (23 percent in the Archdiocese of New York in a 1971 report).[41] Moreover, there was an overall decrease of great proportions in Catholic utilization of the Sacrament of Penance, or confession.[42] As if those factors were not enough to occasion concern about Catholic sacramental life, one also began to see deeper signs of unrest in questions about the very nature of the various sacraments: should children confess before or after first receiving Holy Communion? [43] What is the real nature of the sacrament first called Extreme Unction and now called the Anointing of the Sick? [44] What is the most authentic understanding of and sacramental form for Confirmation, and when and how should it be administered? [45] For anyone who understood the sacraments as fixed in terms of their meanings and forms in life, these questions were alarming indeed, and did nothing but contribute to further malaise and further attrition.

Most Catholics persisted in holding on in rather conventional ways to the sacramental life of the Church. Others looked for something different: another denomination of Christianity, or a religious experience which was not Christian at all, possibly an oriental one. Still others proclaimed Catholic identity without necessarily adhering to standard Catholic patterns of piety in their lives, looking instead for a new outpouring of the Spirit of God in their lives. The "Catholic Pentecostals," who by the early seventies would be found in several hundred clusters across the United States, proclaimed a spirituality that was at once revolutionary, and yet respectful of an essentially conservative Catholicism, seemingly new and yet rooted in the experience of Christianity's first century.

While all of the above emerged as readily identifiable responses to the malaise endemic to Catholic liturgical life in the decade after the reforms of Vatican II and after, there remained a massive bloc of American Catholics who, if they were not enthusiastic about the liturgical program of the Church, at least did not oppose it, and appeared to derive at least a modicum of benefit from it. Others felt that their Christian lives could be lived most meaningfully *alongside* the institutional Church experience of prayer, rather than centered in it. In addition, there appeared here and there pockets of liturgical experimentation (sometimes bordering on liturgical eccentricity) that were

41 See *The National Catholic Reporter*, November 16, 1973, for more recent and thorough national studies.

42 Francis J. Buckley, *I Confess* (Notre Dame, Indiana: Ave Maria Press, 1972).

43 Ibid.

44 *Time*, February 5, 1973, p. 65.

45 Marian J. Bohen, *The Meaning of Confirmation* (New York: Herder & Herder, 1963).

neither totally inside nor totally outside the conventional parameters of American Catholic piety.[46]

What seemed necessary for American Catholics in the area of prayer and liturgy was a serious reexamination of the role of symbols and structures in their worshipping lives. Any full and honest answers to such questioning had to go significantly beyond the trivial concerns of Latin versus English, organ versus guitar, or the various alternative penitential rites and eucharistic prayers in the *Ordo Missae*.[47] There would have to be reconsideration of the parish community (bigger by far than a diocese in early Christian history, in many cases), its role in an age of increasing personal and family mobility, and the role of clergy and laity in its ongoing Christian life. In the meantime, though the reexamination was not forthcoming, there was continuing attrition, as reported somewhat pessimistically by the lay-edited Catholic newsletter *Overview:*

> Mass attendance has always been the lowest common denominator of the faith, but even that indicator continues to fall as the chilly season of lay apathy moves toward a winter not of discontent but of freezing ennui. The lady who last year was saying, "If I hear 'O Sacred Head Surrounded' just one more time," has stopped screaming and is staying home. In a distressingly large number of established parishes, preachers are beginning to hear echoes formerly absorbed by a sea of bodies. And there are fewer fidgeting kids and squalling babies to distract the attention of the steadily aging faithful who do show up. Some of the young people are in the school being worked over by increasing numbers of CCD instructors who are using more imaginative programs and teaching aids to stir their captive audiences, but there are more and more parents whose own casualness about mass-going translates into a feeling of hypocrisy about forcing their kids to swallow a regular dose of Christian doctrine.
>
> Parishes in some new suburbs, especially those around larger cities, show surprising vitality and high levels of parishioner involvement. This atypical but hopeful activity is probably due to the drive of upwardly mobile people who have just escaped from the city's confining and fear-choked atmosphere and rejoice in the chance to get out and try involvement in church affairs. At any rate, they are turning out for talks, meetings, and adult-education seminars that

---

[46] See Edward D. O'Connor, *The Pentecostal Movement in the Catholic Church* (Notre Dame, Indiana: Ave Maria Press, 1971), especially p. 17.

[47] The reference here is to the new "Order of the Mass" issued under the authority of Pope Paul VI for implementation in 1970, after the years of transitional liturgical renewal that have followed immediately upon implementation of the decrees on liturgy emanating from the Second Vatican Council (1962–65).

have long since died on the vine in urban and older suburban parishes. Their CCD programs also flourish and are tied in strongly with social activities for the young.

Meanwhile, many of the former fervid drift in a limbo of shifting small-group involvements and half-hearted worship at liturgies most of them wish were over before they began. Communion in the hand and the occasional trill of a female lector relieve the tedium. In the many places where communal singing has finally died out altogether (the Geritol set prefer to conserve their iron-poor voices to criticize the young priest's sermon), the pastor has exhumed the choir and the voice of the organ is once again heard in the land. Some work hard at developing a suitable lifestyle for disengaged Catholics and hang around the fringes of worthwhile community projects; but they somehow convey and receive the feeling that they do not really belong. All things considered, it's not much fun being a Catholic these days.[48]

Undoubtedly, the cynical view just cited represents the experiences and sentiments of a significant number of American Catholics. Yet many other American Catholics took exception to so dismal an outlook. Some would insist that anyone objecting to conventional Catholic parochial life was ipso facto in danger of being cut off from the very life of the Church and had best be set aright. But this was just a sort of "excommunication approach" that solved nothing save some Catholics' desire for homogeneity. To use the terminology popularized by transactional analysis, it would be tantamount to the conventional institutional Church saying to its individual members, "I'm O.K., you're *not* O.K.!" Yet it would be equally mistaken to assume that, because some Catholics cannot be served by the conventional parochial program, therefore none can, and the whole thing is in need of abandonment or at least amendment. As I suggested in *U.S. Catholic,* in the article "Liturgy for Middle-brows" (May 1973), the American Catholic unable to be served by the parish structure and pattern as we know it may well be but an exception to prove the rule.

To focus light on the subject from another angle, it is necessary to remember that in the history of the modern liturgical movement, and in the present time as well, there is always a danger of expecting too much of the liturgical ritual and the liturgical assembly. In chapter two, we noted a necessary and even salutary diminution in the all-embracing influence of the parish clergy in various facets of American Catholic life, not because the importance of the Church was being downgraded but simply because the Church, once some emergencies had abated, was no longer being expected to perform tasks that it never

---

[48] *Overview,* December 15, 1972.

should have been expected to perform in the first place. So it is, I submit, with the liturgy.

In the earlier days of the liturgical movement, it was supposed that the reform of the Church's liturgy would immediately and perfectly affect not only external ritual and internal spirituality (it has obviously not done either), but also the various aspects of Christian life that would radiate from the Service of the Word (explicating the demands of the Christian Gospel), and the Service of the Eucharist (making present the Body and Blood of Jesus for the acceptance and supernaturalizing of the Church's human members). This would mean, to use a simple analogy, that the revitalized liturgy would be a sort of superfuel for the social apostolate.

This kind of thinking, within a proper perspective, makes some theological sense. The social life of a Christian should indeed radiate from an interior spirituality nurtured by liturgical prayer and sacramental grace. However, the extreme hopes implied in this exaggerated line of reasoning would have us believe that liturgical imperfections would be rectified by official renovations and that human and social imperfections would be rectified by a proper liturgical life. This would not be completely realistic in any era, let alone one in which the influence (at least the appreciable influence) of the Church as institution was becoming less and less manifest. The new presence of the Church in American Catholics' lives was more flexible, more tolerant of different approaches to matters under dispute, and less insistent on lock step uniformity. To suppose that the renewed Church would operate in the same efficient and uniform fashion as the old one would be to suppose a continuation of the very sort of triumphalism [49] that had made the renewed Church so long in coming, and would be tantamount to pouring new wine into old skins, only to see the skins break and the wine spilled. As I observed in *Transformation in Christ* in 1972:

> It used to be felt by many a Catholic that one's own communion with Jesus was all that was needed. . . . To exhibit such an attitude is, of course, to fail to witness to the mystery of Christ as present in the Church or in the world at large, to fail to witness to the oneness of mankind as a race of brothers and sisters having God as their common father. To a large extent, this sort of attitude is being erased from Christian spirituality today. . . . The spokes are all becoming connected quite firmly to the rim.

---

[49] Triumphalism was the spirit, prevalent in the latter stages of the post-Tridentine or Counter-Reformation period in Catholic history (the late sixteenth to early twentieth centuries) which implied that the Catholic Church as institution was so virtually perfect that it need admit no serious internal reform. Triumphalism is said to have died with the Second Vatican Council, though vestiges of it obviously remain.

But there can be another problem here: the connection of the spokes to the rim, but not to the hub. There has been a great tendency of late . . . to become socially involved to an extent which could well put many of yesteryear's Christians to shame, but this often takes place entirely apart from the Christian community. Several observations could be made about this. In the first place, one could certainly opine (as does Karl Rahner in his notion of the "anonymous Christian") that these individuals are indeed Christians doing the work of Christ and his Church, even if they are not conscious of the fact. But that idea, worthwhile though it may be, does not speak to the question at hand in its entirety. The phenomenon is also due, I think, to the fact that the Church is becoming less responsible, *as Church,* for the exigencies of the world. This can be, and probably is in practice, both a good and a bad thing.

The Church, particularly in America, has largely been forced into the context of a subculture. America is officially secular, religionless. Unofficially, particular religions may prevail in the nation generally or in parts thereof. . . . However, Roman Catholicism as a religious point of view or a religious group . . . has never really taken such hold of the life of the community. Even in places where Roman Catholics have seemed to approach a substantial percentage of the population . . . there have always been enough "non-Catholics" to make the Catholics feel as a community apart, sharing in special hardships and special benefits, having their own ways of looking at and speaking about and doing a variety of things.

Thus the development of a Catholic subculture in America, with its own educational system from kindergarten through postdoctoral studies, its own hospitals and social service agencies, its own newspapers. . . , its own youth organizations. . . , its own paramilitary organizations (Catholic War Veterans), insurance aggregations (Catholic Knights of Wisconsin, etc.), fraternal "lodges" (Knights of Columbus and Daughters of Isabella), movie rating systems. . . , groups formed in response to social concerns (Catholic Interracial Council), and so on. This seems to have happened, not because Catholics have a mania for starting or joining organizations, but because Catholics in America were fearful (in some cases, at least for a time, rightly so) that the avenues offered them by the society around them would not suffice for their concerns, or would not be fair with respect to their own particular interests as Catholics. . . . Catholic schools were developed because Catholics felt that they would not be treated fairly in public schools which, for some time, suffered from anti-Catholic bias. Catholic hospitals were founded because the medical needs of Catholics might not be served otherwise. Hostility towards immigrant newcomers to America—Irish, Italian, Polish—made Catholics feel the need to band together, to rally 'round their Church, in ghettoes in many large cities (some of which still exist), and to take care of themselves and their own.

Nowadays, all of American life is far more secularized than before, to the extent that one's religious persuasion entitles him to no special privilege or disfavor, and Catholics need not be so wary as they once were of secular institutions (governmental or otherwise). Many of today's American Catholics feel that their children's religious education can be served without enrolling them in parochial school, and that they will not be made infidels by going to the public school. Many feel that their needs as Catholics and as patients can and will be respected by a gynecologist who is Jewish or a hospital which is Presbyterian. And, in some cases, American Catholics feel that they will fare better for going outside the subculture. They know that, because they have come from the out-group, they will have to be treated fairly, since no one would want to invite charges of inequity.

Part of this is the whole tension between what sociologists call *Gemeinschaft* and *Gesellschaft*: in a *Gemeinschaft* situation, where personal relationships and feelings become the coin of the realm, one can be in great favor or disfavor because of who he is, how he thinks, etc. In a *Gesellschaft* situation, noted and often damned for its impersonal objectivity, no one has to like or agree with an individual, but all must accord him his due rights. The modern American Catholic is now caught in a tension between the preservation of the *Gemeinschaft* values of a religious community and the *Gesellschaft* values that would serve as some sort of "insurance" when the religious community undergoes the sort of turmoil that has been in evidence over the past decade. Many Catholic institutions and structures are now dealing with this tension in ways which in the long run will prove healthy, but many of the Catholics affected by those structures remain to be convinced. In any event, secular institutions and structures (especially the State) are now taking over some of the protective and organizational-social roles which the Church used to have to play in the American Catholic subculture. . . . The individual Catholic today often feels that his involvement in the *saeculum* can take place without the Church, or even despite the Church, when he finds that a good many of his co-religionists do not view the problems, or their solutions, in the same way he does.

Some of the tensions we have described above, then, make *institutional*-Church involvement in "secular" problems both less necessary and less apparent today than in even the recent past. But this situation can be misread by many people, especially many younger people, who tend to feel that the Church should speak univocally on practically every situation. . . . These people are often a bit too young to remember that, not long ago, there was a time when the Church *did* tend to speak univocally on practically every issue, when there

was (or was supposed to be) a clear-cut "Catholic position" on virtually every question. . . .

. . . So it is that today's young Catholic is . . . not led to look to his institutional Church leaders in a paternalistic context, but rather to
act as an individual Christian. . . .[50]

In the above it is expressed that the Church as an institution
is becoming less and less an active force (at least visibly) in the lives of
American Catholics, and that this need not be a bad thing. At the
same time, some observers see that traditional patterns of parochial
worship-life may well continue for some time to come, but that this
will not be anything to boast of if the end result is a lack of growth
in social understanding and identity. Still, as Robert W. Hovda notes,
the type of social identity and understanding necessary for a Christian
community cannot all be expected to be supplied by the liturgy: ". . .
it is folly and totally unrealistic to expect liturgical celebrations to
supply, repair, compensate for all the work which should have preceded
them: faith, conversion, cathechesis, and a community cognizant of
Jesus' message and its mission."[51]

The task for the Catholic Church in America (and elsewhere) will
be to face the fact of diminishing Church influence in a variety of traditionally Church-influenced spheres, all the while not allowing the New
Testament's figurative salt to become insipid.[52] Specifically in the liturgical realm, the Church will need to refrain from imposing on the
liturgy certain expectations which are not really proper to the worship-
life of the Church, while at the same time taking care to ensure that
liturgical life in the Church will be all that it truly can be. I suspect
that this will run against the grain of many Catholics who have been
conditioned by the American ethics of pragmatism and efficiency.[53] After
all, the line of reasoning suggests, why do something if it doesn't necessarily produce results? Why have something if it doesn't work? American
Catholics will have to view their Church afresh, to see their worshipping communities primarily *as* worshipping communities, and not as
centers for a dozen other functions which happen to provide Mass as
well. Moreover, American Catholics will need to view their liturgical
celebrations as primarily directed toward the worship of a God who is

[50] *Transformation in Christ,* pp. 104–9.

[51] Robert W. Hovda, *Living Worship,* quoted in *Overview,* December 15, 1973.

[52] Matt. 5:13.

[53] See Anthony T. Padovano, *American Culture and the Quest for Christ* (New
York: Sheed & Ward, 1970), especially chaps. 1, 2, and 3.

wholly Other,[54] and not somehow meant to meet every specific need. After all, the nature of Christian life and worship would suggest that if a spirituality directed toward worship of the Trinity develops as itself for its own sake, then the satisfaction of numerous human personal needs is apt to follow as well.

In an American Catholic atmosphere of air conditioning, microphones, *Missalettes* all ready to go, and Mass schedules keyed to the parking lot flow, one must seriously wonder how much chance this sort of message has of getting through. If it doesn't, both Catholicism and America are likely to be the poorer for it.

---

[54] I am reflecting the language of Rudolf Otto, in *The Idea of the Holy,* tr. J. W. Harvey (New York: Oxford University Press, 1950), second ed.

# 4

# The One True Church?

One distinctive feature—if not *the* distinctive feature—of Catholicism in America has been the belief of its members that they belong to "the one true Church." We have already seen how such a unique status has at once blessed and burdened the American Catholic with a series of privileges and obligations unknown to the non-Catholics around him.

But we have seen, too, that over the past decade or so, there has been serious emphasis by Catholics and other Christians alike on "ecumenism,"[1] the endeavor to narrow the differences between the various denominations that claim to be Christian in the hope that, witnessing to "one Lord, one faith, one baptism,"[2] these variegated sects might eventually fulfill the prayer attributed to Jesus in the Fourth Gospel, "Father, may they be one in us, as you are in me and I am in you, so that the world may believe it was you who sent me. . . ."[3]

---

[1] Ecumenism means the desire to unite Christian churches. To some, ecumenism also signifies efforts at understanding between Christians and non-Christians. Contrary to a popular misunderstanding, the term "ecumenical" when applied to a Church council, e.g., Vatican II, does not necessarily mean that the purpose of the council is to foster the ecumenical movement, but simply that the council includes representatives of the entire Church, empowered to deliberate as a unified body. See "Decree on Ecumenism," in *The Documents of Vatican II*, ed. Walter M. Abbott, tr. Joseph Gallagher (New York: America Press/Association Press/Guild Press), chaps. 1 and 4.

[2] Eph. 4:5.

[3] John 17:21.

The ecumenical movement in the twentieth century emerged first as an essentially Protestant phenomenon.[4] From a Catholic standpoint, it seemed all right for various Protestant subdivisions to attempt unity among themselves, but not for Catholics to join in. For Catholics to have done so would be to have compromised the uniqueness of "the one true Church" and to have given way to indifferentism, the heretical belief that all Christian sects operating in good faith could claim with practically equal credibility to be authentic transmitters of Jesus' Gospel.[5] Indifferentist thinking implied that any one Christian religion was as good as any other;[6] such ideas were clearly repugnant to any good Catholic, who knew both the truth and the unique character of his divinely established Church against the erroneous sects that had broken off from it or grown up around it. The danger of indifferentism was particularly grave and insidious in the United States, where various religious groups lived and worked alongside one another, and the "one true Church" enjoyed no special protection from the state, as it had in many other countries.[7]

Indeed, there were even further disadvantages for Catholics in America who attempted to preserve their identity. Not only was the American enterprise founded on a religious libertarianism essentially intended for Protestants and not Catholics, but the WASP[8] origins of most Americans did not allow for cordiality toward the later immigrants from Ireland and southern and eastern Europe who were Catholics. The animosity that developed was as much ethnic and sociological as it was religious. Indeed, one could say that more "holy wars" were waged in America over Italian accents and Irish whiskey than over such theological questions as transubstantiation[9] and the various doctrines concerning the Virgin Mary.[10]

Even the earliest of Catholic immigrants into predominantly WASP America,[11] the Irish, experienced being at the bottom of the classic

---

[4] See Samuel McCrea Cavert, "A Response" (to the "Decree on Ecumenism"), in Abbott, *Vatican II*, pp. 367–70.

[5] DS 2915ff.

[6] Ibid.

[7] See Andrew M. Greeley, *The Catholic Experience* (Garden City, N.Y.: Doubleday & Co., Inc., 1967) and John Cogley, *Catholic America* (New York: Dial Press, 1973).

[8] White Anglo-Saxon Protestant, a commonly used pop-sociological term.

[9] The belief that the bread and wine of the Eucharist are transformed in their substance into the body and blood of Jesus Christ at the consecration of the Mass, while retaining the appearances of bread and wine.

[10] E.g., the Immaculate Conception and the Assumption. See DS 2803–4, 3903–4.

[11] See Greeley, *The Catholic Experience,* and Cogley, *Catholic America;* also John B. Duff, *The Irish in the United States* (Belmont, Calif.: Wadsworth, 1971).

immigrant pecking order. One need only recall a grotesque editorial cartoon that appeared in the March 28, 1874 issue of the *Jolly Giant,* published by a San Francisco anti-Catholic bigot, "Colonel" Frank Thistleton: it showed a number of outlandishly ugly and stupid-looking people over the caption "How the Irish Roman Catholics blockade the sidewalk every Sunday, in front of the Jesuits R. C. Church on Market Street, after last Mass." [12] And Irish Catholics in Boston were well acquainted with the job opportunities that were blocked to them by the "NINA" (No Irish Need Apply) signs, the last one of which is said to have been removed from the White House in 1960 with the election of John Fitzgerald Kennedy.[13]

The Irish may actually have had an ultimately easier time of it than some Catholic immigrants who came later. The Irish, after all, generally understood English, and their names were not so foreign to the Anglo-Saxon ear (although Sean often became John, and Seamus James in the New World). For the Italians, the Polish, and other southern and eastern Europeans, the barriers were not only religious and ethnic, but also linguistic, and more profoundly racial. They were even, to some extent, maintained by the Irish who came before. Perhaps the Italian and Polish experience of discrimination resembles that of the Irish far less than it resembles that of yesterday's Jews or today's Hispanic-American Catholics, whose very faces and names indicate a different racial strain, and for whom American English must usually be learned as a second language.[14]

Because of the ethnic tensions that were endemic to the immigrant experience, being Catholic in America meant something different from being Catholic anyplace else. There was no easy homogeneity in spite of the shared religion. As Steven V. Roberts observed, as recently as 1970, in *The New York Times Magazine:* "In Bayonne (New Jersey), ecumenism is when the Polish speak to the Italians." [15] In many sectors of the United States, one ethnic group was quick to emphasize how well it kept the faith, contrasting this to the failings, impieties, and aberrations of its Catholic neighbors from another background. An American Catholic who knew anything of the "old country" directly,

---

12 Associated Students, University of San Francisco, *The 1961 Don,* ed. L.D. Vandendale (San Francisco: University of San Francisco, 1961), Golden Jubilee Edition, p. 172. Also see John B. McGloin, *Jesuits by the Golden Gate* (San Francisco: University of San Francisco Press, 1973), pp. 1–21 and *Eloquent Indian: The Life of James Bouchard, California Jesuit* (Palo Alto: Stanford University Press, 1949) for additional historical background.

13 Greeley, *Catholic Experience,* chap. 7.

14 Ibid.

15 *The New York Times Magazine,* December 6, 1970, p. 43.

or who had learned of it vicariously as part of a common racial memory,[16] was apt to perceive the differences between his own brand of Catholicism and those practiced by his coreligionists of different national origins, and it would seem to him a compromise of the unity of "the one true Church" that these differences should be allowed to exist alongside what he considered his own pristine version of Catholic faith and practice. The "ethnic Catholics" of America do realize that there is less to be gained in opposing each other than in confronting whatever common adversaries may exist. This does not suggest that the Irish, the Polish, the Italians, and more recently the Puerto Rican and Chicano Catholics, will not oppose one another in a variety of intramural political and ecclesiastical struggles. (In New Jersey, both Essex and Hudson counties have afforded textbook cases of such rivalry, and others can be found elsewhere.) But it does mean that they see the sense of banding together in matters of Catholic concern amidst a secular society—the civil questions of abortion laws, State and Federal aid to private education, etc.—and in proclamations of their Catholic identity in that larger society—Holy Name parades and Good Friday observance campaigns in the fairly recent past, even the St. Patrick's Day parades in New York, San Francisco, Boston, and elsewhere.

The American Catholic feeling of isolation and suspicion might be characterized by this story out of my own experience: In early 1965, shortly after I had moved into an apartment on the western fringe of Newark, my parents came to visit. My father looked through my livingroom window at the view which extended across the city and over the Hudson to the Manhattan skyline. As he spied an Oriental-looking structure looming up from the nearer regions of Vailsburg he asked, "What's that place?" I explained that it was St. John's Ukrainian Catholic Church, at Sandford and Ivy. "Oh," he said, "it's a national parish." "No," I took pains to point out, "it's Eastern Rite." "I see," he replied, "like the Greek Orthodox." "No," I answered, "they're Uniate; that is, they. . ." In sincere exasperation, my father broke in, "Look, all I want to know is—are they one of us or aren't they?" I submit that in light of this kind of question all data about ecumenical endeavors involving American Catholics must be assessed.

The various ethnic groups that were set off from their fellow Americans not only by nationality but also by religious denomination grew up in America learning all sorts of things about who they were—things that should be peripheral in any authentic religious vision, but which for

---

[16] That is, a memory which an individual possesses as a member of a race or group, even if not directly but only vicariously, such as Jewish consciousness of the Exodus/Covenant experience in the thirteenth century before Christ. See George Devine, *Why Read the Old Testament?* (Chicago: Claretian Publications, 1966).

a long time seemed to be at the focal point of their self-understanding. For the Irish it was important to note that "We have the *real* Mass, in Latin, while the Protestants have only a make-believe Mass in English!" Against such a background, it is not hard to understand the initial resistance of American Catholics—particularly Irish-American Catholics—to the liturgical reforms heralded by the Second Vatican Council. For the Italians or the Polish, and later for the influx of Hispanic-American Catholics, there were other things: Our Lady of Guadalupe, or Festa San Gennaro, or kielbasy at Easter sometimes seemed almost as important as the Eucharistic Presence, or in any case more tangible and intelligible.

When it was announced that there would be an ecumenical council, many "ethnic Catholics" in America would have no part of it. After all, if "ecumenical" meant getting together with the Protestants (which, in the case of the phrase "ecumenical council," it did not) [17] then it could come to no good. "And all the changes coming from that ecumenical council! English in the Mass, less emphasis on devotion to Mary, more stress on the Bible, laymen in the sanctuary—These are just ways of selling our Church out to the Protestants! If that's what 'ecumenical' means, then real Catholics want no part of it." [18]

Anyone who understands the history of the Roman Catholic Church in the long view, including the years of the Second Vatican Council (1962–65), will be quick to realize that the reforms initiated or announced by the Council had no purpose or effect other than to make the Church adhere more closely to authentic *Roman Catholic* tradition, which in many instances might happily converge with Protestant witness to the same Lord, faith and baptism.[19] In this connection, it would only be by becoming more authentically and integrally Catholic that the Roman Church could enter into any sort of meaningful or productive dialogue with the "separated brethren." [20]

But many "ethnic Catholics" in the United States would be hard put to realize this. Not out of the hardness of their hearts was this the case; if anything, they were people capable of demonstrating exemplary generosity in the name of the Church and its mission in the world, and often an almost stupefying obedience to their bishops and pastors in executing the detailed movements of that mission as it was entrusted to

---

17 See fn. 1.

18 This is a paraphrase of a Catholic attitude frequently expressed during the 1960s. See Elaine F. Tyhanic, "What Makes a Catholic Conservative Conservative?" *Catholic World*, July, 1966.

19 Eph. 4:5.

20 A term commonly used, since the advent of ecumenism, in Roman Catholic circles, to describe those commonly referred to previously as heretics or by the purely negative designation "non-Catholics."

them. But too much of "this ecumenical business" seemed altogether foreign to them, could not ring true, and smacked of a sacrifice or compromise of what they had labored to build and defend as a Catholic fortress in Protestant America.

The reasons for the shock became apparent only after too much of the painful impact had been indelibly registered in numerous sectors of the American Catholic subculture. It was obvious that for all too long the faithful in Catholic America had received a religious education which had inadvertently confused the substance of the faith with its incidentals, the essential revelation with the most superficial of outer wrappings, and the very Barque of Peter with the smallest of its barnacles.[21] Abstinence from meat on Friday became not a disciplinary application of a penitential spirit, but both a burden and a badge for the American Catholics who would proudly order their separate meatless entrees at business and social functions. The Roman liturgy became a distinction from the WASPs for any American Catholic, and the jibes like "Benny's got all the dominoes!"[22] would often be answered by the sneering joke that Episcopalians were nothing more than would-be Catholics who had flunked Latin. The celibate priesthood became an incarnate resolution not to emulate men who had allegedly "started their own churches" owing to their marital wants. (As recently as the late 1950s, Catholic schoolchildren were commonly told that Anglicanism was sustained only by Henry VIII's desire to divorce and remarry, and that the whole Protestant Reformation began simply because Martin Luther wanted to leave the Augustinian order of priests and marry a nun.)

By the time careful historical and theological scholarship had prepared the scholarly and pastoral leadership in the Catholic Church for the internal renewal that was to characterize and be characterized by the Second Vatican Council, it became apparent how muddled some of our previous religious education had been. But by then it was already too late to change for many American Catholics, and many sincere efforts to "reeducate" or "update" them failed ineptly in the face of so massive an obstacle. The very intramural renewal of the Roman Church was up against this obstacle, and to a large extent still is. It should be no wonder that any sort of serious ecumenism dare not entertain hopes of faring dramatically well at the outset.

---

[21] The image of the Barque (ship) of Peter is one of many symbols of the Church in Catholic tradition. See Robert Blair Kaiser, *Pope, Council and World* (New York: MacMillan and Co., 1963), chap. 1.

[22] A parody of the phrase *Benedicamus Domino* (let us bless the Lord) used as the dismissal versicle of the Mass at various points in the liturgical year in the Roman Rite according to the Tridentine *Ordo Missae*, e.g., Lent.

Therefore by the early 1970s American Catholicism had done little beyond the stage of what I call "coffee and doughnut ecumenism." This is the sort of encounter typified by insipid declarations of common ground—"Why, *we* believe in the Trinity, too! See how much we have in common?"—when the participants are too unsure of themselves and each other to venture further into areas which may be problematic. Such exchanges take place infrequently (often during the Church Unity Octave or around Reformation Sunday) [23] and with the social assistance of many doughnuts and cups of coffee. If the truth be told, the doughnuts are often unnecessary, so abundant is the excessive sweetness at such gatherings. This is not to imply that the Church, on her higher levels of ecclesiastical and intellectual leadership, has yet to make serious ecumenical progress, or that there do not exist edifying examples of Catholic ecumenical activity. It is to point out, though, that Catholics in America generally feel uncomfortable with their own changed and changing Church, let alone with the "separated brethren," and are thus incapable of much beyond the stage of polite initial encounters, however often these polite initial encounters may repeat from scratch.

The picture sketched here refers especially to coastal Catholicism, that is either on the East Coast, where immigrant Catholics have come directly from the "old country" and settled and reproduced in clusters, or in California, where many immigrant Catholics settled, coming from across the Atlantic without being appreciably touched by the American heartland. (My great-grandfather, like many San Francisco immigrants, stopped on the East Coast en route from Ireland, in New Haven in his case, then worked his way around Cape Horn on board a ship.) In the Midwestern United States, by contrast, the picture seems somewhat different, at least in degree.

Writing for an *America* magazine symposium on "Catholicism Midwest Style" in 1966, Andrew M. Greeley noted that ". . . for all its unquestioned faults, the Mid-American Church has . . . adjusted much more rapidly to the challenges of the New World and will probably adjust with greater enthusiasm to the opportunities of the New Church in an ecumenical age." [24] In support of his thesis Greeley stated that

> . . . in the East, Catholics are often a majority but are tempted to act and think like a minority, while in Mid-America, they are a mi-

---

[23] The Church Unity Octave is celebrated from the eighteenth to the twenty-fifth of January each year by Catholics, between the feasts of the Chair of Peter and the Conversion of St. Paul, according to the Roman liturgical calendar. Reformation Sunday is traditionally the last Sunday in October among Lutherans and many other Protestants. In ages past, such observances tended to be denominationally self-righteous; today, they afford occasions for ecumenical exchange and fellowship.

[24] Andrew M. Greeley, in "Catholicism Midwest Style" (A Symposium), *America* 114:7 (February 12, 1966), p. 223.

nority who are quite unaware that they are a minority and often think and act like a majority.

Catholic immigrants arriving in New York and Boston found a stable and well-established society that was not particularly eager to let them in. . . .

In Chicago, St. Paul, and St. Louis, on the other hand, Catholics were on the scene in relatively impressive numbers from almost the beginning. It was not someone else's society, but ours as much as anyone else's. . . .[25]

John W. Padberg, writing for the same symposium, made similar observations: "The Catholic Midwest earlier ceased to equate the faith with the particular practices of special immigrant groups, and so, with a greater serenity than would otherwise have been possible, it could innovate." [26] Some of this, opined Justus George Lawler in the same context, may be due to ". . . the transition (in episcopal power) of St. Louis from Glennon to Ritter, of St. Paul from Murray and Brady to Binz, of Chicago and Milwaukee from Stritch to Meyer, that is, in the transition from an Irish to a non-Irish bishop. . . ." [27] Although some obvious changes have taken place since the time of which Lawler wrote in 1966, one could still understand his distinction of the Midwest from "the major sees in East and West . . . governed by prelates of Irish extraction." [28] Lest Lawler's remarks be taken as ethnic slurs, he explains:

This should not necessarily lead one to conclude that the American Irish are congenitally more reactionary than the non-Irish. The reasons are deeper than that and probably have to do with the fact that the Irish, more discriminated against than other 19th-century immigrants, could guarantee their social rights neither by wealth nor property nor the respect of their Protestant neighbors, but only by close alliance with local politicians. Such an alliance, it is clear, militates against any radical social apostolate. Non-Irish Catholics— the Germans because of lack of prejudice against them, the Italians and Slavs because municipal caesaropapism had been preempted by the Irish—unable or unwanting to cultivate this union of throne and altar, were free to develop their own instruments for social improvement, and for the improvement of their environment.

Lastly, it should be said that these thumbnail Spenglerisms are already obsolescent as succeeding generations of Catholics, whether Irish, German, Slavic or Latin, abandon the folkways of their elders. These

---

25 Ibid.
26 Ibid., p. 227.
27 Ibid., pp. 227f.
28 Ibid.

are patterns from the era of the Kennedys and the Cushings—a very
old-fashioned era. . . ." [29]

There may be something to what Lawler and his colleagues in the
symposium have said concerning the Catholicism that is not essentially
coastal, as that found in San Francisco, New York, Philadelphia, and
so on, but which is thriving alongside its neighbors without fear of
being stamped out or, perhaps worse, ignored to the point of impotence.
In that vast stretch of more flexible turf between the Alleghenies and
the Sierra Nevada, ethnicity seems blurred, and there are few St. Patrick's
Day parades or pizzerias, only a seemingly endless procession of flatlands
dotted with neuter establishments such as Exxon stations and McDonald's
hamburger stands. In his attempt at a historical novel, *The Sandbox
Tree*, Thomas Fleming seems to feel the same way about Mid-America.
As the story ends, his heroine Margaret Connolly, who had been brought
up in a strict East Coast Irish Catholic family and a stringent convent
college, runs away to marry her Protestant boyfriend. As they leave
together on their journey, Fleming concludes his story by telling the
reader, "In minutes they were on the turnpike rolling west, the yellow
lamps stretching ahead of them into the heart of America." [30]

In an epilogue to the same story, Fleming tells us of correspondence
he has received from Margaret, as a way of helping explain the import
of his novel and its implications:

> "We were married by a Justice of the Peace in Ohio, where we
> stopped while Dick negotiated . . . a loan. . . . We honeymooned in
> motels between there and Denver. That's where we decided to live. . . .
> I explained it all to my mother by mail. There was a lot of hysteria
> in the first few letters, but after a year or so, she calmed down, and
> even came out to visit. She died about five years ago, Daddy about
> five years before that.
>
> "Dick and I both love Denver. It isn't perfect—what city is?—but it
> has that western sense of community that makes you proud to par-
> ticipate in charity drives and other kinds of civic causes. . . .
>
> "The Church? I just stopped going, when I married Dick. I knew he
> could not stomach it. I faced that, on the ride to the shore, that last
> night. I faced so many things that last night! But it was amazingly
> easy, once the facing began. It had all been *constructed,* so it seemed
> then, so that an absolute choice was the only way. So I chose.
>
> "I haven't built Dick up into a god or anything like that, as a sub-

---

[29] Ibid.

[30] Thomas Fleming, *The Sandbox Tree* (New York: William Morrow and Company, 1970), p. 404.

stitute. We've just lived a life together, a loving life. I still believe in a God that (I'm borrowing from Dick here) it is arrogance to define. Occasionally we go to the Unitarian church in our suburb. Our children . . . go to public schools. But I feel closer to God when we go skiing . . . than I ever feel (or will feel, I guess) in church. . . .

"In one of your last letters, you asked me if the new or post-Vatican II Catholic Church . . . has made it easier for me. I can see that you can't get that old adage, once a Catholic, always a Catholic, out of your head. It is obviously almost impossible to convince you that no matter what the Church did or said, or will do or will say in the future, it simply no longer matters to me. I've become something else—something better, I think: a free, adult American.

"But I don't worship America instead of God. I just mean that by choosing freedom, with Dick's help, I was able to escape that claustrophobic Catholic world that almost swallowed me. I say this as matter-of-factly as possible, without any bitterness, because by going away as we did, I was able to escape most of the personal recrimination and social ostracism that my apostasy—to use an old-fashioned word—would have brought me in the city of my birth. . . ." [31]

Some would quickly dismiss Fleming's letters from Margaret as unbelievable. To suppose that the rigors of East Coast Irish Catholicism, with the vocational urgings and sexual hangups of a college chaplain, would be sufficient to propel a young girl rather instantly into a life-long separation from her roots is to give these factors far more credit than they deserve, in my own opinion and that of some others.[32] Margaret may be a convenient vehicle for Fleming's own social theses, but as a literary character she is ultimately difficult to lend credence to. Fleming is right, in the same epilogue, when he notes that ". . . the sententious historian is endangering the novelist." [33]

Fleming concludes his book by quoting from another of his characters, Judge Kilpatrick: *"Who the hell asked you to shed tears for us? We didn't ask for anybody's pity. . . . Let's end it that way."* [34]

To dismiss coastal Catholicism as being so influenced by the "old country" as to be not genuinely American makes about as much sense as Spiro Agnew's celebrated attempt in 1969 to disenfranchise (at least rhetorically) New York from the Republic. It is precisely the spices of the North Beach section of San Francisco, the Cuban colony in Union

---

[31] Ibid., pp. 405–7.

[32] See my remarks and those of William J. Toohey in *The National Catholic Reporter*, November 16, 1973, p. 15.

[33] Fleming, *The Sandbox Tree*, p. 408.

[34] Ibid.

City, N. J., the South Sides of Chicago and Milwaukee (two Mid-American
cities with large Polish colonies), and even the little Italian enclave in
New York's East Harlem that make up the flavor known as "American."
To take them away would be to render the end product insipid beyond
recognition, leaving us with a "culture" which is at best contrived and
artificial, like the half-time show at the Orange Bowl game. As Glazer,
Moynihan, Novak, and others have reminded us, the "ethnics" will not
go away; they will not even "melt." Fleming's fictional Judge Kilpatrick
recognizes this, and this is why he wants no pity. He only wishes others
would be canny enough to recognize it also. Moreover, today's observers
are beginning to reject the "melting pot" imagery. My own alternative
is the analogy of a stewpot, wherein each flavorful chunk of meat,
vegetable, or potato remains whole unto itself, adding to the overall
flavor of the potion.

Hispanic-American Catholics seem to be realizing this concretely,
if for no other reason than that "white" Catholic America insists on
isolating them to such an extent as it does. Thus we have seen movements like *Catolicos por la Raza,* and bishops like Patrick Flores of San
Antonio. Black Catholics in America are following suit with the National Office for Black Catholics and in the persons of such leaders as
Lawrence Lucas and Joseph Davis. The Italians and the Polish are not
far behind. While this sort of thing may appear divisive at first, it may
be the only possible process for the survival of all the things that give
both America and American Catholicism their vitality.

The Irish, who got here before most other American Catholics, are
rather ironically in danger of missing the boat, as Greeley suggests:

> The American Irish are in a most unusual position. For the first time
> in the history of American society, it is legitimate to be an ethnic.
> Black pride has become acceptable, even obligatory, for American
> blacks. The Chicanos and the American Indians are right behind
> them proclaiming pride in their traditions. If black is beautiful, and
> if red is beautiful, the children and grandchildren of the immigrants
> are asking why they should not think the same way. Polish is beauti-
> ful, Hungarian is beautiful, Italian is beautiful, Greek is beautiful; in
> Chicago, even Luxembourger is beautiful. One may not only be pub-
> licly proud of one's heritage on certain days of the year; one can be
> proud every day of the year. Nay, increasingly, one *must* be proud.
> He who does not have any racial or ethnic tradition to fall back upon
> is forced to stand by in shamed silence. If you are neither black nor
> ethnic, how can you be part of the black-ethnic dialogue? One con-
> fidently expects the dawn of the day when some New England
> prophet will announce that Yankee is beautiful.
>
> But in the midst of all this resurgence of ethnic pride, the state

of the Irish is distressful (to use their word), indeed. At long last, it would be legitimate for them to act as if they were Irish.

Only they've forgotten how.

The legitimation of ethnicity came too late for the American Irish. They are the only one of the European immigrant groups to have over-acculturated. They stopped being Irish the day before it became all right to be Irish. The WASP's won the battle to convert the Irish into WASP's just before the announcement came that permanent peace had been made with ethnic diversity. . . .[35]

By believing and seeking to achieve the superficial aspects of the "American Dream," the Irish and others alike stand in danger of losing their very souls and hearts and identities. If this appears at first preposterous, follow the fleshing-out of Greeley's thesis:

> . . . if James T. Farrell (author of *Studs Lonigan*) had grown up at 93rd and Hoyne instead of 57th and Indiana (in Chicago, i.e., in an upper-middle-class suburban-type neighborhood as opposed to the old Irish neighborhood), he would never have set a word on paper. What are the rest of the potential storytellers doing? Why, they're pushing their careers, investing in the stock market, vacationing in Mexico, playing golf at the "club," drinking martinis and watching professional football on Sunday afternoons. . . .[36]

And for such observers as Greeley, the prize has not been worth the effort:

> The temptation proved irresistible. You could sit by the bog and dream, so long as respectability was not a real possibility. But in the United States, the Irishman finally found an opportunity to be accepted—though not fully, of course, by the "real world" of the Anglo-Saxon. Aided and abetted by his mother and his priest he set out to prove definitively that he was just as good as anyone else, if not a little bit better. Unfortunately, he succeeded.

> But respectability has always meant something very lower middle class for an Irishman, even if he owns a steel mill. The Irishman's concept of respectability is shaped by the narrow parochialism of the "lace curtain"—probably because most of his aristocrats long since went over to the enemy. The sad truth is that the Irish new rich do not really know how to spend their money and their idea of "class" and "style" rarely exceeds flying to Dallas to watch Notre Dame play in the Cotton Bowl.[37]

---

[35] Andrew M. Greeley, "The Last of the American Irish Fade Away," *The New York Times Magazine*, March 14, 1971, pp. 32–33.

[36] Ibid., p. 53.

[37] Ibid., p. 54.

Thus, for the second or third generation of immigrant Catholic Americans, the trophy is only brass and its display is often boorish and tawdry. Moreover, the pedestal on which the trophy stands is usually frightfully precarious, as is seen in the tendency of so many "ethnics" to shed their roots. As Greeley narrates in the opening of the same article:

> Not so long ago I was wandering through the halls of a progressive Catholic women's college with a young woman I know and noticed a sign announcing that the Irish Club was to meet that afternoon.
>
> "Are you a member of the club, Peggy?" I asked.
>
> "A member? I'm the president!"
>
> "And what do you do at your meetings?"
>
> "Why, we plan the St. Patrick's Night Ball."
>
> "Peg, have you ever heard of the Easter Rising?" She had not.
>
> "And, Peg, what about the Sinn Fein?" She thought it might be Chinese.
>
> "And, what's the Irish Republican Army?" As a loyal Cook County Democrat, she wanted no part of it.
>
> Finally, "Peg, who is Eamon de Valera?"
>
> "Oh, I know! He's the Jewish man who's Mayor of Dublin."
>
> And so the last of the American Irish fade away into the mist. . . .[38]

This tendency will not be limited to the Irish, though commentators like Greeley, Moynihan, Breslin, and Hamill and novelists like Cullinan, Sheed, and Fleming have made them the textbook case. The same thing will be seen, to be sure, in many San Francisco Italians who make the move to the Sunset district or the Peninsula, often forsaking the community and identity of neighborhoods like North Beach. It will also be seen in some Polish and German Catholics who cut off the ties of their communities in cities like Chicago, Milwaukee, and Philadelphia. It will be seen in immigrants of all strains who flee the old New York neighborhoods to find homes with finished basements in Queens or on Staten Island. The writers and producers of the popular movie *Joe* (1970) did not say so and perhaps they did not have to, but their title character is the epitome of the second- or even third-generation Catholic immigrant who feels he has just "made it," in very limited terms, and is scared to death that whatever he has "made" will be unmade. In the sterile neighborhoods of the Sunset district, Queens, the Jersey suburbs, and the Peninsula, as well as 93rd and Hoyne, the veneer of recent

---

38 Ibid., p. 32.

acculturation and assimilation is often applied unevenly and roughly over a suppressed and self-denigrated identity, and as a result all that remains of some Catholics' ethnic identity are stupidities like green beer and "Kiss Me, I'm Italian" buttons, and people who say "dese, dem, and dose" but mock the failure of Puerto Ricans and southern Blacks to "speak American." In short, the end result has often been the worst of both worlds.

So it is that the American Catholic of recent immigrant status at first embraced his Church as a vehicle for his own upward mobility, but then questioned it when it turned its attention toward justice for *other* minority groups. And although it is the fashion for a stage bigot to pick on *all* minorities, one suspects that any credible analysis of television's Archie Bunker, who lives off Northern Boulevard in eastern Queens, would reveal his religious affiliation could be Roman Catholic as likely as Protestant. Further research would probably show that his surname could have Gaelic roots or could have been Anglicized from its original Italian or Eastern European form. A glance at any ecclesiastical map of the Diocese of Brooklyn could probably tell you what his parish is. And interestingly enough, it is in heavily Catholic neighborhoods like Bayside, Rosedale, and others, that Archie has his greatest concentration of fans. In one part of Queens, they even named a bar after him.

This sort of individual, both singly and in numbers, would feel threatened not only by members of different racial or ethnic groups, but by other religions as well, and would have reason to remember examples of anti-Catholic discrimination—real and exaggerated—in his own experiences or those of his ancestors in this country. As a defense mechanism, a Catholic American of this type would pride himself on the Faith, the ingredient that made him superior to the others around him. So it came to pass that insecurity and defensiveness conflated in the religious, ethnic, racial, and socio-economic spheres, generating *groups* of peoples in Catholic America [39] who were terribly suspicious of and nervously self-righteous against "them."

The examples do not limit themselves, of course, to extreme characters like Joe and Archie Bunker. They can be found in sedate, upper-middle-class suburbs like those in New Jersey, where a semichic young woman asked me after a lecture, "What is there left to being a Catholic, now that we've come down so far in our religion? We have the Mass in English, we no longer keep the fasts, and so many other things have been relaxed. Our religion used to have so much more to it, but now

---

[39] I am using this phrase here as John Cogley means it, to denote a sub- or counter-culture, as in his book *Catholic America*, q.v.

we've come down to the level of the Protestants!" [40] And as Midwesterners like Greeley well know, examples can also be found in Mid-America, especially in cities large enough to develop ethnic pockets. I recall, for example, a German Catholic in Milwaukee who once considered my allegiance to the Church questionable since I ate dinner in the cafeteria at the YMCA.[41]

It is this sort of thing against which the ecumenical movement in the American Church must work, and which prompts Greeley to wonder, "What if American Catholicism had been presided over by more Irishmen like John England, who democratized his diocese in 1825, or John Ireland, who preached and practiced ecumenism in 1890—long before even the word was invented?" [42]

It became evident, before long, that ecumenism, including both Protestant-Catholic and even Judaeo-Christian relations, could never succeed among American Catholics unless it could be made clear to them that they were not only not in danger of losing, but that they would indeed gain, from rapport with other Christians and ultimately with members of all other religions. This gut-issue, on all its levels, will decide the future of Catholic participation in ecumenical affairs far more profoundly than decrees of councils, statements from the Vatican, or the zealous ecumenical activities of local Church authorities, however necessary those supports might be to keep alive the ecumenical movement. As attested by Vatican II's decree on ecumenism:

> Cooperation among all Christians vividly expresses that bond which already unites them, and it sets in clearer relief the features of Christ the Servant. Such cooperation, which has already begun in many countries, should be ever increasingly developed, particularly in regions where a social and technical evolution is taking place. It should contribute to a just appreciation of the dignity of the human person, the promotion of the blessings of peace, the application of gospel principles to social life, and the advancement of the arts and sciences in a Christian spirit. Christians should also work together in the use of every possible means to relieve the afflictions of our times, such as famine and natural disasters, illiteracy and poverty, lack of housing, and the unequal distribution of wealth. Through

---

[40] This is a paraphrase, but a rather faithful one, of the lady's remarks. The lecture and subsequent remarks took place at St. Mary's Parish in Dumont, New Jersey, in 1971.

[41] The year was 1963. At this time, and for some time thereafter, it was commonly believed by American Catholics that any form of support, however indirect, for an organization that was generically Christian and not specifically Catholic was tantamount to tacit support for the heresy of indifferentism, i.e., the belief that one Christian religion was as good as another. See fn. 5.

[42] Greeley, "The Last of the American Irish Fade Away," p. 58.

such cooperation, all believers in Christ are able to learn easily how they can understand each other better and esteem each other more, and how the road to the unity of Christians may be made smooth.[43]

If Roman Catholics in large numbers have been unresponsive to the imperatives of ecumenism, American Protestants have also faced disappointment in this area as well, as seen in the recent setbacks and reassessments that have come for the Consultation on Church Union,[44] whose General Secretary, Rev. Dr. Paul A. Crow, Jr., still insisted:

> Whatever may be the difficulties and obstacles, God still calls the churches to unite. The same Gospel unmistakably calls us to fuller unity/union; obedience to the message of Christian mercy and love is beyond our reach without a fully committed fellowship. Even more now than twelve years ago (when Dr. Eugene Carson Blake issued a call for unity among four Protestant denominations), the realities of our daily world call us to the ministry of reconciliation. In America we are a nation of strangers. A current public poll reveals 41 percent of all Americans feel alienated from people and the structures of society these days. The church's primary task of mission and evangelism still cannot be completed without unity/union. God still wills that his people shall be visibly and recognizably one in order to bring the world to its peace and unity in Christ, who is head not only of the church but of all mankind. He wills for the church to be the pilgrim company of the whole human race redeemed in Christ, and which anticipates and partially realizes the kingdom of God among men. Yes, this vision has been tested again, and I do not believe God has changed his mind.[45]

As time went on, it became apparent that ecumenical progress in America, and particularly Catholic involvement in this progress, had to include the understanding and respecting of differences of identity, and not the glossing over of them. This would, hopefully, lead ultimately to an atmosphere of mutual self-respect among religions and respect for one's partners in the endeavor, rather than the sort of Alphonse-and-Gaston charades that seemed so satisfactory in the first years of American Catholic ecumenical activity. To a large extent, American Catholic contributions and responses to a healthy ecumenical movement

---

[43] Walter M. Abbott, ed., *Vatican II*, p. 355.

[44] See Edward B. Fiske, *The New York Times,* April 8, 1973, Section 4, "The Week in Review," p. 9, col. 1.

[45] Paul A. Crow, Jr., "If Not the Reunion of Christ's Church—Then What?" (Princeton, N.J.: Consultation on Church Union, 1973), a sermon delivered at Grace Cathedral (Episcopal), San Francisco, California, December 3, 1972, p. 3.

will depend on various individuals and groups within Catholic America developing more secure self-images and more assertive lives, rather than just desiring assimilation into their idea of WASP America, for this has brought them so much self-destruction. It will depend, moreover, on long term grass-roots sharing of religious insight and witness. All appearances indicate that the first must be a prerequisite to the second. It will be, we now can tell, as long a process as it will be worthwhile.[46]

---

[46] Note the role of theological consortia in this regard, as in my article "Seminaries: 'Fortress' Days Are No More," in *The New York Times*, February 4, 1973, Section 4, "The Week in Review," p. 9, col. 4.

# 5

# A "New Morality" for Catholics?

One of the most frequently used phrases among Catholics in America has been "faith and morals." The phrase has a specific theological application (delimiting the subjects on which a pope may speak infallibly for the Church, that is, matters of faith and morals),[1] but it also underscores a basic Catholic belief that certain moral courses of action will necessarily follow from certain religious beliefs. In the atmosphere of interdenominational suspicion that infected Christians before the advent of the modern ecumenical movement, Catholics often misunderstood Luther's teaching to mean that faith alone was sufficient for salvation, without regard to what one *did* about his faith (one's "works"). Luther didn't teach that, of course, any more than did Paul, whom Luther was citing,[2] as Catholics would come to realize in time,[3] but one can easily understand how a Catholic would be repulsed at any suggestion that one's works were of negligible importance in the practice of religion. For Catholics there has always been strong emphasis not only on what one *believes,* but on how one *acts* in the moral sphere.

---

1 DS 3073–4.

2 Paul had distinguished in Romans 3:27–31; 4:1–25 between faith in Jesus and the mechanical performance of works of the (Mosaic) Law. Luther later reiterated the distinction, allowing for inclusion of mechanical performance of legalistic obligations generally, all the while understanding faith (*fides*) as a faithfulness to Jesus, from which good moral actions of necessity would follow. See also Gal. 2:16.

3 Harry McSorley, *Luther: Right or Wrong?* (Minneapolis: Augsburg, 1969).

This is not to suggest that all Catholics lead lives which are morally blameless, any more than to suggest that all Catholics understand in depth such doctrines as the Eucharistic Presence or the Assumption, which they profess. But in "faith and morals," they understood that the rules had been clearly laid down—this is what one believes, and this is how one acts in order to be a good Catholic. Any shortcoming or failure was clearly identifiable and in need of reparation.

In such a light, it is not hard to envision the anxiety with which an average Catholic would view any change in the actions he would be expected to perform in living out his faith-commitment in the Church. Even the relatively minor observances of liturgical ritual—the fast before Holy Communion, abstaining from meat on Fridays (and under certain other circumstances), fasting during Lent (and, again, under certain other circumstances) [4]—had been taught to Catholics within the framework of possible punishment, often "under pain of mortal sin." [5] This sort of emphasis not only ensured widespread fear of transgressing such rules (which, fortunately, were not terribly difficult to keep), but also made their substance appear to have a certain moral character (which, apart from the moral obligation to obey Church authority, they did not; they were practices of devotion). Such a simplistic view of ecclesiastical obligations tended to work most efficiently for an era wherein Catholic practice did not appear to undergo any appreciable change: right was right, wrong was wrong, and the two were clearly labeled, although mortal sins were distinguished from lesser offenses. Eating meat on a Friday was wrong, and so was murder. Missing Mass on Sunday or a holy day of obligation was a mortal sin, and so was adultery. The celebration of Mass in any language except Latin was forbidden, and so were other things that were also wrong (even if not mortally sinful): the reading of Scripture in the sanctuary by a layman (let alone a *laywoman!*), the use of contraceptives identified by the

---

[4] E.g., vigils of some feasts, Ember days, etc. See chap. 1.

[5] Unrepented "mortal" (serious) sin would occasion eternal damnation. The phrase "under pain of mortal sin" is a term used by moral theologians. Canon Law indicates that a matter is of serious obligation by using other terms or words. Thus in the matter of fast and abstinence the words used are *vetat, servanda est, praescribit* CIC, Cans. 1250, 1251, 1252). The term used for Sundays and holy days of obligation is *Dies festi sub praecepto* (Cans. 1247, 1248). The heading under which the material above is treated in the Code of Canon Law is Book III, Section II. The Canon (18) which is most useful in matters of interpretation states, as translated: If the words of the law, in the text and context are clear, they are the sole norm of interpretation. Only in case the text remains obscure may recourse be had to the other norms of interpretation, i.e., parallel passages of the Code, the purpose and circumstance of the Law, the mind or intention of the legislator. (For his advice in these and other matters of Canon Law, I am indebted to Rev. Msgr. Alexander F. Sokolich, J.C.D., a Canon lawyer of the Archdiocese of Newark, and sometime professor at Seton Hall University.)

Church as artificial,[6] liturgical music using profane instruments like guitars and banjos,[7] marriage for the ordained or ordination for the married,[8] and so on.

The seminary professor, the wise confessor, the skilled preacher or religion teacher, and the thoughtful layman all recognized, of course, the various degrees of gravity involved in the various matters just described. To suggest that Catholic teaching really meant to blur the distinction between the offense involved in taking another human life and the offense involved in eating a hot dog on Friday would be a grossly unfair caricature of the Church. However, when all these things came home to roost psychologically and emotionally, many lay Catholics combined them in the same general category: rules of the Church which should not be broken.

It was true that the Church could dispense from some of these obligations. If a feast day fell on a Friday (that of the Patron of the Archdiocese, for example), the bishop might dispense from the obligation to abstain from meat. St. Patrick's day was usually grounds for dispensation from fast and abstinence during Lent in any diocese housing even a few Irish Catholics.[9] Moreover, the alert Catholic knew in the back of his mind that other rules made by human authorities in the Church could be bent or even broken by human authorities in the Church—even matters of such import as the Latin Mass [10] and the celibate clergy that had prevailed for so long in the Roman Church. However, many Catholics always thought that even things like fasting

---

6 This would mean all methods of contraception excepting abstinence from intercourse, either complete or periodic (the "rhythm method"). See Robert G. Hoyt, ed., *The Birth Control Debate* (Kansas City, Mo.: NCR, 1969).

7 See William J. Leonard, ed., *The Instruction for American Pastors on Sacred Music and the Sacred Liturgy* (Boston: McLaughlin and Reilly, Inc., 1959). This was the prevailing document on the subject until the promulgation of Vatican II's Constitution on the Sacred Liturgy (*Sacrosanctum Concilium*, 1963) and subsequent instructions. Instruments other than the organ were allowed for by competent local authority (i.e., the bishop, or by way of delegation his commissions on sacred music or the sacred liturgy), but "profane" instruments like the guitar and banjo were probably not included in the permission.

8 The Roman Church has for centuries forbidden both the ordination of married men to priesthood (except by way of a most extraordinary dispensation) or the marriage of a priest. This does not obtain in the Eastern Rites, however. Since Roman or other Western Rite Catholics account for about 96 percent of the total membership of the Catholic Church, the prohibitions are widespread among the world's Catholics.

9 This reflects the older discipline of fast and abstinence.

10 The use of Latin in the Mass actually arose as the result of a vernacularist trend (away from Greek) in the Western Church between the second and fourth centuries A.D., then was crystallized from the decree of Pepin in 754 (with some exceptions) until the Second Vatican Council's *Sacrosanctum Concilium* at the end of 1963. See my detailed description of this in *Liturgical Renewal: An Agonizing Reappraisal* (Staten Island, N.Y.: Alba House, 1973).

and abstinence (except in special dispensations as mentioned above) simply did not change, and if these did not change, then matters of greater weight in the moral order were surely even less subject to possible adaptation, as these clearly came not from human ecclesiastical authority, but only *through* that authority from God.

Thus Catholic morality was difficult and at the same time easy. It might be difficult to *carry out* one's obligations in the Church, but at least it was always easy to know what the obligations were. In this regard, Catholics surely considered themselves more fortunate than the Protestants, who were left in the uncertainty of "private interpretation." One's own interpretation in one's conscience, after all, could easily be wrong, but if the Church did the interpreting and spelling out of moral obligation for its members, it would be taken care of not only with dispatch but also with great precision. To be a Catholic, up until the early 1960s, meant that "you knew where you stood." You knew what you had to do and what you had to avoid.

A large measure of Catholics' having known where they stood for many years, up until the time of the Second Vatican Council, was achieved by a catechetical process which sought to convey all the obligations of a Catholic, with all the attendant penalties for disobedience, without always taking care to distinguish between different levels of gravity or inflexibility. This was an attempt at a religious education on a grand scale which (as I wrote in *To Be A Man,* 1969) "sincerely attempted to communicate wholly the faith life of Christ's Church, but which often seems to have made the mistake of articulating the accidental just (or almost) as forcefully as the substantial—Latin in the Mass and no meat on Friday with the Blessed Trinity and the Virgin Birth." [11]

With this background, one can appreciate how even the slightest adjustments in routine practice (the external conduct of the liturgy, for one obvious example) caused many Catholics to feel that they no longer "knew where they stood." Moreover, since so many of these previous obligations had been communicated in the frame of reference of what Catholics must do or not do under pain of sin,[12] one can likewise appreciate how many Catholics felt that their Church was in some way shifting its moral posture, even if this was not actually the case.

If it was now permissible to celebrate the Mass in English and to eat meat on Fridays, many Catholics began to wonder, what was happen-

---

[11] George Devine, ed., *To Be A Man* (Englewood Cliffs, N.J.: Prentice-Hall, Inc., 1969), p. 6.

[12] In many cases, the obligation was under pain of lesser (venial) sin.

ing to morality? Would it now become all right to use contraceptives previously condemned by the Church? Would priests be allowed to marry? Would the Church cease its strong opposition to premarital sex or to divorce and remarriage? In truth, there were no logical connections to support such questions, but there surely were strong *psychological* connections: the seemingly changeless Church, even in some rather small ways, had changed.[13]

There was another dynamic at work. The Catholic Church, which until the early 1960s had tended to stress morality in terms of individual obligations ("saving one's own soul," etc.), now began to emphasize social obligations in the moral order. Part of this was renewed emphasis on the Pauline doctrine of the Church as a *corporate* reality (the Body of Christ),[14] with *interdependent* members. Another dimension of this, to some extent pursuant to the first, was papal emphasis on the moral principles of the Gospel as applied to a host of social and economic questions, which were treated in a number of "social encyclicals" [15] by Pope Leo XIII, then Pius XI, and more recently John XXIII and Paul VI.[16] From the pulpit and in their confessionals, priests were beginning to emphasize morality as social or communal. There were even communal celebrations of the Sacrament of Penance (confession), lending further stress to this realization among Catholics.[17] The type of new approach to moral responsibility for Catholics which began to take hold around the time of the Second Vatican Council was well summed up some time before the Council by the theologian, A.-M. Roguet:

> Our approach to the sacrament of Penance will be quite different if we look upon it from the point of view of our life in the com-

---

[13] Garry Wills, in chapters 1 and 2 of *Bare Ruined Choirs: Doubt, Prophecy and Radical Religion* (Garden City, N.Y.: Doubleday & Co., Inc., 1972), suggests that the difficulties are due in large part to the fact that Catholics were *unaware* of changes going on throughout the Church's long history. His view is that, just as sex (existent in reality, but seldom acknowledged) was the Victorians' "dirty little secret," change was the Church's "dirty little secret."

[14] 1 Cor. 12. This came to be called the doctrine of the *mystical* body of Christ in Scholastic theological language, which distinguished the Church from other types of bodies (e.g., physical and moral). Its re-emphasis in modern times is often identified with Pope Pius XII's encyclical letter *Mystici Corporis Christi*, AAS XXXV (1943) 193–248.

[15] So called because they take the form of an encyclical letter circulated by the Pope as head of the episcopal college to his fellow bishops, and because they deal with questions in the social order. For some treatment of the social encyclicals' impact on twentieth-century Catholics, see Wills, *Bare Ruined Choirs*, especially chapters 2 and 3.

[16] See Charles E. Curran, "Roman Catholic Social Ethics: Past, Present and Future," in George Devine, ed., *That They May Live: Theological Reflections on the Quality of Life* (Staten Island, N.Y.: Alba House, 1972), pp. 87–122.

[17] See Devine, *Liturgical Renewal*, chap. 7.

munity. Too many Catholics, always ready to make allowances in their own favour, find that they have committed hardly any sins. This is because they restrict their examination of conscience to the commandments of God and the Church which they might have transgressed formally. Since they have not committed murder or theft they can find only simply material little sins, not too humiliating, such as . . . being late for Sunday Mass. Realize your solidarity with your neighbour, and remember that the first, if not the only, commandment is that of fraternal charity; that you are not only required to work out your own salvation but that you are also responsible in the eyes of God for . . . your fellow Christians and the advancement of the kingdom of God. Now you will find something to confess. . . .[18]

If the various movements affecting Catholic consciousness of sin and reconciliation had all converged smoothly, we would surely have been the beneficiaries of a new social moral consciousness, a slow and silent death for scrupulosity and excessive legalism, and at the same time a salutary preservation of a strong sense of personal individual moral obligation and interior religious and moral discipline. And all of these would have been elements of an appreciable maturation of Catholics individually and as a community of faith and practice. Unfortunately, as with many other aspects of Catholic life in America and elsewhere during the turbulent 1960s and the years immediately following, the gears ground, emitting a maddening screeching sound which would make it well nigh impossible for anyone to hear the voice of reason.

It is worth remembering what Roguet pointed out: Catholics have for too long been preoccupied with "simply material little sins, not too humiliating." [19] When Catholic teaching of religious discipline, in the wake of Vatican Council II, began to de-emphasize "material little sins," like the regulations concerning fast and abstinence,[20] this was done in the context of a hope for a deeper understanding of personal morality in light of the social demands of the Gospel. The Church earnestly hoped that individual Catholics would now pay less heed to questions of fast, abstinence, and other "material little sins," and more attention to the

---

18 A.-M. Roguet, *Christ Acts Through Sacraments* (Collegeville, Minn.: The Liturgical Press, 1954), p. 94.

19 Ibid.

20 Until this was relaxed in American dioceses in the late 1960s, Catholics in America were normally required to abstain from meat on Fridays and on the vigils of (days before) certain feasts during the liturgical year, and to observe fasts according to prescribed norms during Lent and at other specified times. The obligation to abstain from meat on Fridays during Lent was still imposed by many dioceses in the United States by the early 1970s.

social teachings of Popes Leo XIII, Pius XI, John XXIII, and Paul VI, who had spent much time in the late nineteenth century and the twentieth century outlining the applications of Christian social morality to the changing exigencies of modern times.

However, as with many other aspects of Catholic faith and practice, and contrary to popular caricatures of Roman Catholicism, the entire Catholic world does not catch pneumonia—does not necessarily even catch cold—when Rome sneezes. This was seen, toward the end of the 1960s, in the case of Paul VI's encyclical letter *Humanae vitae* pertaining to birth control.[21] It should have been seen earlier by the alert observer with regard to the "social encyclicals," even the celebrated *Mater et Magistra*[22] and *Pacem in Terris*[23] of Good Pope John. But in the early 1960s, it was too often gratuitously presumed that any shift in official policy at the top of the Catholic pyramid would be followed to the letter all the way down to the base. This assumption was perhaps an accurate reflection of official Catholic views concerning authority and obedience in "faith and morals," and in even such less central matters as the mode of celebrating the liturgy or observing the penitential seasons.[24] It was, however, inaccurate in terms of people's abilities to adequately understand, not just notionally but on a deeper existential level, all that was being said to them and demanded of them. Moreover, it is one thing to assent in theory to a teaching of the Church (including those teachings which, like the social encyclicals, did not claim the papal prerogative of speaking infallibly for the Church),[25] and quite another thing to act in perfect accord with that teaching. The Church has long recognized and made provision for the fact of human sinfulness and man's lack of perfect compliance with the Word and will of God.

Yet there is more to it, in honest terms. The "old morality" would endure—even if weakened and amended—because the "old morality" was *easier*. Its legalisms allowed any Catholic to "know where he stood" and to understand his moral obligations in terms of "material little sins" that were "not too humiliating" and perhaps rather comfortable to deal with. Accordingly, many Catholic confessionals, discussion groups, parlor conversations, and classrooms from primary grades through college would devote far more time and energy to the laws for fast and abstinence, the moral ratings of movies according to the Legion of De-

---

21 AAS LX (1968): 481–503. See Hoyt, ed., *The Birth Control Debate*.
22 AAS LIII (1961): 401–64.
23 AAS LV (1963): 257–304.
24 See fn. 20.
25 See fn. 1.

cency,[26] the obligation to attend Mass every Sunday and holy day,[27] and similar questions than to the ramifications óf underdeveloped nations, labor and management, world peace, and race relations. As a case in point, I recall my senior year as an undergraduate at the University of San Francisco. I had enrolled in an elective course in advanced public speaking. The Jesuit instructor [28] announced at the beginning of the term that all of our exercises in exposition, oratory, discussion, and debate would be drawn from the source materials of the social encyclicals, and he told us, "If you don't get it in this course, I'm afraid you won't get it in any other!" He was right. The year was hardly before the papal social encyclicals became popular among Catholic intellectuals; it was 1962.[29] Moreover, the University was (in my experience) at least as advanced as most Catholic colleges in the United States for its attention to contemporary theological and moral issues and their social implications. USF was considered unique for its study of communism [30] (required of each baccalaureate candidate), but the course was in fact a negatively oriented approach rather than a positive

---

26 The Legion of Decency later became known as the National Catholic Office for Motion Pictures (NCOMP) and rated movies in terms of their moral content as to suitability for viewing by Catholics (distinguishing between adults, adolescents and children). Its function became somewhat peripheral in American Catholic life when the general moral rigorism typical of American Catholicism tended to ease up in the late 1960s, and when the MPAA effected its own code of ratings (GP, G, PG, M, R, X). Contrary to popular Catholic opinion, the Legion never represented official teachings of the Church in its ratings, and compliance with its recommendations was not a moral obligation for Catholics (I was severely criticized by some of the more defensive Jesuits at Marquette University for suggesting this in a letter to the *Marquette Tribune* in 1964). See chap. 1, fn. 41.

27 Holy days of obligation, when the Mass obligation is the same as that of a Sunday, are fixed differently for various countries. In the United States, the holy days that were established by the hierarchy are January 1 (the Solemnity of the Mother of God), Ascension Thursday (forty days after Easter), August 15 (the Assumption of the Blessed Virgin Mary), November 1 (the Feast of All Saints), December 8 (the Feast of the Immaculate Conception, and December 25 (the Feast of the Nativity of Jesus, Christmas).

28 Rev. James J. Dempsey, S.J., of the Department of Communication Arts.

29 See Wills, *Bare Ruined Choirs*, chap. 8.

30 The course, PoliSci 140, was a vigorously ¹aught and rigorously documented attack on communism for its atheism and also its economic policies and political effects. One of its good points was that it required students to read works they might not otherwise have read (e.g., Marx's *Communist Manifesto*). The course was devised and conducted by Rev. Raymond T. Feely, S. J., Professor of Political Science, who was an early student of Marxism and its philosophical, social, and political implications. Father Feely was also the author of the "Credo" of the University of San Francisco, which spelled out the University's commitment to a number of Christian and American principles, in matters ranging from the sanctity of marriages and the family to the obligations of labor and management to cooperate in the establishment of a just socio-economic order in the world. For the historical background of PoliSci 140, see John B. McGloin, *Jesuits by the Golden Gate* (University of San Francisco Press, 1973), pp. 221–22.

approach to what was recommended by the Gospel. This is an example how Catholic moral instruction was often characterized, more by what it condemned than by what it encouraged.

If Catholic moral teaching was characterized more by the prohibitions of the Gospel than by the imperatives of Christian moral obligation, then Catholic moral consciousness seemed burdened with almost innumerable taboos. Even positive commands appeared to be negative ones: "Remember the sabbath day and keep it holy" [31] became "Thou shalt not miss Mass on a Sunday or holy day of obligation or thou shalt be guilty of mortal sin"; [32] reverential fast before Communion was read as "Thou shalt not take solid or liquid nourishment except water, save in instances of illness, for three hours before Communion"; and even "Honor thy father and thy mother" [33] was remembered as "Thou shalt not disobey legitimate authorities—especially ecclesiastical ones!"

Quite understandably, there existed an atmosphere wherein the removal of any prohibition or taboo would be a most welcome development, but the very relief itself would occupy center stage, rather than the reasons for it. When fast and abstinence regulations were relaxed, in keeping with the renewed Church's desire for less legalism and greater stress on interior penitential spirit, all that most Catholics saw was the lifting of a burden, and not a shift in modes of expressing penitence. American Catholics in general were quick to read the headlines telling them they need no longer forsake meat on Fridays or for Lenten lunches, but failed to see the fine print reminding them they were obliged to adopt penitential attitudes and actions in other ways that would be more meaningful to them personally and more productive for the human community at large.

As implied before, when American Catholics got a glimpse of diminishing moral and ritual prohibitions, they began to wonder whether their heaviest obligations might be lifted. Almost too predictably, yet in a very sudden and painfully awkward way, American Catholics' attention turned in the mid- and late 1960s to sex. It is by now a matter of public record and even of artistic celebration [34] that sexual

---

[31] Exod. 20:11. The decalogue was never meant to be a guide for Christian morality *per se,* and is really just one ingredient of the Mosaic Law. However, the ten commandments have come to be known as a handy way of categorizing chief areas of moral and ritual obligation for Christians, and so have been "borrowed."

[32] Concerning the popular Catholic notion of the Mass obligation "under pain of mortal sin," see Msgr. Raymond Bosler's column, the "Question Box" in *The Advocate* in several issues through the early 1970s, and in other Catholic newspapers around the United States around the same dates.

[33] Exod. 20:12.

[34] See John L'Heureux, *The Clang Birds* (New York: The MacMillan Company, 1972).

prohibitions have been a favorite hang-up for Catholics, especially American Catholics under a predominantly Irish influence. Given sex as a great gift, they were so afraid of its being misused or spoiled that they concentrated more on the possibilities of misusing it than they should have, and not enough on the possibilities for its proper use. As a result, an atmosphere of sexual repression was created that was at most somewhat efficient for "keeping people out of trouble" and for avoiding sexual excess. But it was all part of a superstructure which could not operate flexibly, and once the atmosphere of flexibility was introduced, the superstructure's rigid character was not able to allow for or tolerate it. The principle implied is the one every San Franciscan knows from the 1906 earthquake: the old wooden frame house with a lot of "give" to it is apt to survive a severe shock better than a more formidable and rigid structure.[35] As a result, once the superstructure was shaken by the vernacularization of the liturgy, the introduction of previously "profane" musical expression into worship, and an apparent "laicization" of religious-order garb as well as the relaxing of penitential observances, one of the first elements to be shaken loose was one of the heaviest and one of those least able to roll with the shocks and aftershocks: the rigid ways which American Catholics had devised for viewing, understanding, and dealing with human sexuality. At its silliest extremes, this phenomenon manifested itself in the 63-year-old Dominican sister in New York who sought dispensation from her vows "in order to marry" or the 53-year-old monsignor in California who did the same, so convinced were they that they had been bamboozled into forsaking something essential to their personhood, and that they had best regain it quickly.[36]

In more conventional arenas of conflict, many married Catholics would insist that their conjugal relations no longer had to be justified in every instance by openness to progeny, and an increasing number would consider the prohibition of "artificial contraception" by Popes Pius XI, Pius XII, and even John XXIII and Paul VI, irrelevant to their Catholic lives in the Sacrament of Matrimony. At the same time, many anxious young Catholics who, a few years before, would have waited until marriage to experience sexual intimacy, now felt that to forego intercourse until achievement of a permanent and exclusive

---

35 Whether or not Eastern investors who have built in San Francisco are shrewd enough to have grasped this fact will be demonstrated by the ongoing activity of the San Andreas fault.

36 The sister, after a year's search for a husband and bitter disappointment, sought and received readmission to her community. The monsignor's fiancée changed her mind about him and, after having burned his ecclesiastical bridges behind him, he reportedly went insane.

relationship would only make them, once more, the victims of a Church which appeared unable to make up its mind. With a vengeance, in many cases, they set about making up for enough time already lost.[37]

There was a widespread sexual immaturity among Catholics in America, perhaps not much different in nature, but quite different in symptoms, from the sexual immaturity that had existed *before* the mid-1960s, and it resembled on the surface the sexual immaturity of Americans in general. This was the kind of giggling schoolchild approach that made *Playboy* [38] possible and the "working at sex" that Rollo May termed a "new puritanism" [39] for its inability to realize what Gregory Baum knew about symbols—that they are not really symbols if you have to explain them in detail [40]—and what Graham Greene knew about sex in particular—that it is neither solemn nor dull.[41] Throughout it all, American Catholics felt less than totally comfortable with the new games, and when not playing too hard at them, they often sought the same sort of labyrinthine rationalizations to support their actions that they sought a decade before to argue against them. (In this context, I once wrote, a theology professor in a Catholic college who could offer an argument in favor of premarital sex was apt to become as popular as free beer at a picnic.[42]) Previously, American Catholics, even if they had not always acted according to Church teachings about sex in the past, had at least always known and externally assented to such teachings in a reassuringly uniform manner.[43] Now the reassuring uniformity seemed gone, and in its place were the nagging questions, "When is it right and when is it wrong?" and "All right, but what about *this* case?"

Difficult situations have a way of conflating in the most perplexing of combinations, and now other areas of moral concern for Catholics became equally problematic around the same time. Just as so many of the old certainties were being threatened in the areas of personal belief, ritual, and morality, there arrived on the scene an experience that signified one more threat to traditional ways of understanding and reacting

---

[37] See Andrew M. Greeley and William McCready in *America* 127:334–37, October 28, 1972.

[38] See Park Honan, "The Sad, Fat *Playboy* of an Urban Society," *New City*, June 1963.

[39] See May's chapter in Michael J. Taylor, ed., *Sex: Thoughts for Contemporary Christians* (Garden City, N.Y.: Doubleday & Co., Inc., 1972).

[40] See Baum's essay in George Devine, ed., *New Dimensions in Religious Experience* (Staten Island, N.Y.: Alba House, 1971).

[41] See Graham Greene, *May We Borrow Your Husband?* (Harmondsworth, Middlesex, England: Penguin Books, Ltd., 1969).

[42] "Catholic Higher Education: Two Views," *Catholic Currents*, January 15, 1972.

[43] For an example of "old school" Catholic teachings on sexual morality, see George A. Kelly, *Modern Youth and Chastity* (St. Louis: The Queen's Work, 1943).

to things (not only for Catholics in this case, but for all Americans): Vietnam. American Catholics knew from their catechisms and their college textbooks in ethics [44] that there was always the possibility of an unjust war, but they felt that most wars were just and necessary. Moreover they believed that the United States only fought just wars in the first place. Whenever the call to arms was sounded in America, Catholic citizens were at least as quick as anyone else to rally 'round the flag; indeed, as the saying goes, to "wrap the cross in the flag," in spite of the unfair slurs against Catholics as "disloyal," "not fully American," or "committed to a foreign prince in Rome." No group among Americans surpassed Catholics for constancy of devotion to their country and defense of the homeland. The presidential election of John F. Kennedy had removed the last barrier to ascendancy for Catholics in America, and it had been bought with the blood of countless American Catholics in defense of this country (Kennedy's older brother among them). Now suddenly many Americans—including Catholics—were raising their voices in protest against the conduct of what they called an immoral war in Vietnam. Some of them were even priests, brothers, and nuns! For many American Catholics, these last were immediately discredited as religious leaders, but for quite a few others it was not so simple a matter. Here was food for thought. Perhaps the war in Vietnam *was* immoral. Perhaps the cleric (or lay Catholic) who said so was more Catholic and American, not less. In any case, one more certainty—or virtual certainty—was going by the boards. When, American Catholics wanted to know, is a war just and when is it unjust? Whatever the textbooks had answered in the past, it appeared that they hadn't anticipated the moral perplexities of Vietnam.

There arose other moral dilemmas for Catholics in America. The Church, for so long the advocate or champion of lower class white immigrants from Ireland, Italy, and eastern Europe (particularly Poland), was now appearing to change and was becoming the advocate of Catholic immigrants to California and the Southwest from Mexico, and to New York and other northeastern cities from Puerto Rico. This was often in direct conflict with the interests of white American Catholics, who formed a part of what Cesar Chavez called the "agribusiness" empire in California and who were accused of being the oppressors (in politics, education, law enforcement, and in economic facets of life) of Hispanic-Americans in the East. Many American Catholics began to resent the extensive dedication of some Church leaders and agencies to a "Spanish-speaking apostolate," when they felt they had not had the benefit of being considered a special "Italian-speaking" or "Polish-speaking" apostolate on *their*

---

[44] E.g., Austin Fagothey, *Right and Reason* (St. Louis: Mosby, 1963).

hard way up the ladder in the new country. Not only that, but the Church was starting to reach out to the Blacks—and most of them were not Catholics but Baptists or members of some other non-Catholic sect (perhaps even Black Muslims). If the Church was calling upon her members to embrace these "Johnnies-come-lately," it appeared to them a strange sort of moral justice indeed.

Briefly, the average American Catholic no longer "knew where he stood," and the staggeringly complex and rigid superstructure of certain moral questions-and-answers seemed gone, probably to stay gone for good. Nothing could hope to duplicate it, but something would have to replace it.

One obvious attempt that was made was to reiterate traditional understandings of Catholic moral consciousness, not only in essential matters but even in some woefully trivial regards of external ritual. This sort of thing, clearly, would be doomed from the outset, and could count as adherents only a handful of people, often in the senior citizen generation, who acted more out of insecurity than out of moral understanding and conviction. These were usually sincerely concerned Catholics, but their tragic flaws were unnecessary rigidity and nearsightedness. They would continue to campaign against pornography and to insist that women cover their heads when going to church, yet not see racism. One wonders if a more gradual change in external ritual might have allowed these people to view Catholic moral priorities more sensibly and to make a more positive contribution to this aspect of the American Church's life.

Seemingly close to this type, but in reality significantly different, were those who, in the name of "Catholic tradition," would seek to preserve a hypocritical sort of moral schizophrenia which, although it transcended denominational lines, picked up specifically Catholic manifestations. These people would read the New York *Daily News* for both its right-wing editorials and its center-spread photos of the biggest-bosomed secretary on all of Wall Street. They would likely read *Playboy* as well, yet have plastic statuettes of the Blessed Virgin on the dashboards of their pollution-belching status symbols from Detroit. Four-letter words would punctuate their private conversations, yet they would consider them "obscene" anywhere else—"nigger" and "spick" and "whop," however, would be quite all right. They would wear American flags in their lapels, and cheat on their income taxes. In their defense of "traditional moral values" they would have one set of obligations for themselves and another for everyone else, yet they did have a strange, primitive sense of fair play not unlike that found on a Little League diamond. In a moral sense, these people are children, but children who many times are half a century old and in need of a parental influence from the Church: a careful combination of firmness and tenderness, to obtain at least a modicum of tangible result and growth. But the Church, at least for quite some time after the upheavals of the middle and late 1960s, was hardly in a position for moral leadership. Moreover, the American instinct for pragmatism and for immediately verifiable results —which is as much Catholic as it is Presbyterian or Jewish in the United States—would begin to find little argument in favor of the Catholic Church as moral instructor. The old Catholic morality of "sex justified by procreation," or at least of prohibiting contraception,[45] had been put to the test and found wanting in the psychological, emotional, and physical lives of millions of married Catholics. The new morality of "Love thy neighbor" and "We shall overcome" has been put to the test and found wanting in the streets of Newark, Detroit, Los Angeles, and Milwaukee. If ever there was a time for the Church to persuasively and effectively solve a moral problem simply by issuing a proclamation, this was not it.

Meanwhile, American Catholics were beginning to realize that the moral positions of the Church had not all been handed down at Creation, or at Sinai, even upon or immediately following the events of Jesus' earthly ministry and the giving of the Holy Spirit to vivify the Church at Pentecost. Rather, the Church's understandings of some moral issues had *developed,* as professors like John T. Noonan would demonstrate in the instance of usury.[46] Further, even the seemingly immutable "natural moral law," that cornerstone of Catholic college courses in ethics, which all rational men and not just men of faith were able to know, might admit of exception or development.[47] In short, any moral understanding which was authentically Catholic would have to be

---

[45] "Sex justified by procreation" is somewhat a caricature, albeit a popular one, of Catholic teaching on sexual matters. It is refuted by even that most conservative of Catholic sources, the Code of Canon Law, which makes impotence (the inability to have sexual intercourse) an impediment to marriage, but does not so treat sterility (the inability to procreate, even if the ability to copulate remains undisturbed). [CIC, Can. 1068.] The prohibition of contraception has been seen by many as based on a Catholic view of "sex justified by procreation"; however, my view is that Catholic arguments on this issue are essentially based on other premises, i.e., interpretation of natural moral law. See Hoyt, *The Birth Control Debate.*

[46] This is the position of Charles Curran on natural law, as reflected in a lecture he gave to the College Theology Society (New York Region) at St. John's University (Jamaica) in 1967. The moral absolutes, so-called, envisioned by natural law, are generally qualified by the phrase *ut in pluribus* (in most cases), according to Curran. Also cf. Curran's book of essays, *Contemporary Issues in Moral Theology* (Notre Dame, Ind.: Fides, 1970).

[47] See John T. Noonan, Jr., "Making One's Own Act Another's," in George Devine, ed., *A World More Human, A Church More Christian* (Staten Island, N.Y.: Alba House, 1973), pp. 145–58, and "Authority, Usury and Contraception," *Insight* 6 (Fall, 1967), 29–42.

grounded in the Gospel and would have to find support in the tradition of the Church, but would not necessarily be unchanged from its first articulation, nor would it necessarily be inflexible. For most Catholics, this view could not afford them the sort of certainty to which they had become accustomed.

Many Catholics, in the middle of the decade just past, became quite interested in "situation ethics," as expressed primarily by Prof. Joseph Fletcher and later by his Catholic colleague, Thomas A. Wassmer. At first, "situation ethics" became attractive to sophomores as a vehicle for justifying their latest sexual misdeed, real or contemplated. Upon closer examination, "situation ethics" is far more complex than a simple procedure for exempting oneself from general moral principles. Fletcher insisted, in first exposing his thoughts on the subject, that an action was not morally good or evil in itself, by its nature, but only in the context of its situation or circumstances, in terms of whether it was a loving (therefore morally good) or nonloving (therefore morally evil) act.[48] Dominican priest Herbert McCabe, in a famous debate in the pages of *Commonweal,* had to challenge Fletcher's thesis by asking, in effect, "How do I *know* if my action is morally good or evil, i.e., is loving or not?" Father McCabe's question, paraphrased here, implies that we humans are quite capable of deceiving ourselves, particularly if we do so in our own favor.[49] Following McCabe, but not ignoring the strong points of Fletcher, I have argued that:

> . . . all human experiences and circumstances are truly unique. However, human situations often enjoy enough similarity (all births, all deaths, all first loves, all homecomings, etc., have such a general similarity to each other that they can be described by these very generic terms) that they can be imitated or not, endorsed or not for others who will come later, as "the thing to do" or "the thing not to do." So that we can say that a particular type of action, *in general,* is or is not worthy of emulation. Thus we cannot simply say that (a given) situation is so awfully unique as to defy its classification as a moral action *in itself,* i.e., in the objective order, apart from whatever mitigating circumstances might arise from the psyche or surroundings. . . .
>
> I would think that, if we gave sufficient thought to the question, we would generally agree that taking the lives of one's wife and children is, at least in general, not a good thing to do, circumstances notwithstanding. And I suspect that most of us would be quite willing to

---

48 See Joseph Fletcher, "Love is the Only Measure," and Herbert McCabe, "The Validity of Absolutes," in *Commonweal* 83:14 (January 14, 1966), pp. 427–32.

49 Ibid., pp. 432–37.

make this a principle, however implicit, for the conduct of our lives, and perhaps even those of others as well.

So we *are* led to talking of objectively right or wrong moral actions, all the while admitting that circumstances may diminish or even eliminate personal (subjective) moral responsibility or guilt for an objectively wrong action.[50]

Wassmer, after some time passed to allow for reflection on the original impact of Fletcher's theses, argued that situational considerations would make it more difficult, not easier, for a Christian to apply the moral imperatives of the Gospel to particular cases. "Situation ethics" demands that one follow one's conscience, Wassmer says, not simply in what one's conscience says one *may* do, but more importantly in what one's conscience says one *must* do.[51] If we are to seek examples of this in Christian tradition, St. Thomas More immediately comes to mind: he did not actively seek martyrdom (if he had, his attempt would have been vain and counterproductive), but found himself a martyr since he found in conscience no moral alternative.[52] An approach to moral questions which is at least to some extent situational is surely indicated by the present moral perplexities facing Catholics, but the example of Thomas More (among others) tells us that this has in some way been part and parcel of Catholic morality all along.[53] And, as implied above, it is literally the sophomore alone [54] who can envision a situational approach (providing all the proper evidence is duly considered) as an "easy way out." Compared with the complex but reassuring jungle gym of categories and formulas that had seemed to be immutably certain, it necessarily means a way that is neither easy *nor* out. But the weakening of the joints and the rusting of some of the supports in the jungle gym means that children over six years of age will now use it only at their own great personal risk. In other words, an approach to moral questions which, while applying sound moral norms, is complex, and at least in some measure situational, has been thrust upon American Catholics whether American Catholics are ready for it or not. If the Church at its middle management levels (the hierarchy in the United States, the Catholic press, and religious education teachers of all sorts) is ready to engage the American Catholic populace in becoming more ready, then a

[50] George Devine, *Transformation in Christ* (Staten Island, N.Y.: Alba House, 1972), pp. 123–24.

[51] See Thomas A. Wassmer, "Contemporary Situational Morality and the Catholic Christian" in *To Be A Man*.

[52] Robert Bolt, *A Man for All Seasons* (New York: Random House, 1962).

[53] See Vatican Council II's Declaration on Religious Freedom, #3.

[54] Sophomore, from the Greek, literally means "wise fool."

truly Catholic moral consciousness may be seen emerging, to the benefit of Americans in general and to the credit of the Catholic Church in America, especially in terms of the social imperatives of Christian moral principles. If not, then the losses which the Church as a moral guide has sustained over the last decade and more will probably only multiply to the point where, for all its internal sincerity and vigor, the moral force of the Catholic Church in America will be hard put to appear to Catholics and Americans in general as anything more than sounding brass and tinkling cymbals.

# 6

# Where Do We Go from Here?

The surveys taken of various facets of contemporary American Catholicism in the previous chapters of this book have necessarily been brief and rather general. Brevity and generality would be even more manifest in any attempt to "play the prophet." But there are some questions worth asking and some tentative answers worth offering, when we wonder what might be some of the future directions for Catholics as a group in America in the remaining quarter of the twentieth century and perhaps for some time thereafter.

If any one observation is essential at the outset, it is this: our ability to generalize about Catholics and Catholicism in America is far less certain than it would have been even in the early 1960s. The reasons for this have been indicated in previous chapters of this book, in terms of a series of challenges to the American Catholic identity in myriad areas —clergy-laity relations, liturgy and prayer life, morality as regards diverse questions such as sexuality and war and peace—which hoped to occasion a rather serious reexamination of just what the American Catholic identity is, or if one is clearly discernible at all. The reexamination as we have seen it take place over the past decade and more has been such that different American Catholics, in different life situations and environments, dealing with different questions and speaking from various vantage points, have come up with answers that are not necessarily contradictory but surely quite diverse. If we ask the question, "*Is* there such a thing as an American Catholic identity?" I submit that the answer cannot be a simple *yes* or *no;* rather, it must be that there are a number of different perceptions of "the American Catholic identity" which have emerged in the turbulent decade since the Second Vatican Council.

It is worth noting here that the terms "Catholic" and "American" have a certain similarity in that they are both meant to be understood quite broadly. This makes them difficult terms to deal with when we are seeking specific definitions. We are always in danger of so strongly emphasizing one manifestation of "Americanism," or Catholicism, that we fail to acknowledge others which may be equally legitimate even if less obvious. Too often we try to deal with this dilemma by defining the terms negatively, for example, by what is *not* Catholic, or what is *not* American. Here we must be exceedingly careful, lest we exclude elements which we have no right to exclude. Many Americans will likely recall the controversial role of the House Un-American Activities Committee in the 1950s, and even younger Americans may remember when the Vice President of the United States, in 1969, committed the faux pas of suggesting that the "eastern liberal establishment" was somehow not as truly American as the people in the heartland who happened to agree with the policies of the current administration.[1]

If we understand words like "American" and "Americanism" *essentially* (in what formally constitutes the foundations for these terms), we will necessarily see a Puerto Rican picnic at Orchard Beach in the Bronx, a luau in Honolulu, or a bratwurst feastival in Wisconsin as every bit as American as Anita Bryant singing "God Bless America" on television. At the same time, those of us who savor the different flavors which various racial, national, and ethnic groups have contributed to the American stewpot[2] are in danger of denigrating the Anita Bryant kind of Americanism for lacking genuineness. It may be synthetic and artificially homogenized, but it is American, nonetheless. We should realize that if we ourselves are at all American, our own Americanism is indeed genuine and protected only if we honor the legitimacy of other Americans' ways of life and expression. Only when we see clear evidence of something which threatens the very nature of Americanism (for instance, refusal to afford equal protection under law as guaranteed in the Constitution) do we have grounds to contrast persons or actions that are faithful to America and Americanism with those that are not.

This analogy also applies to Catholicism. The people in the suburbs

---

[1] This was the famous "media speech" of Vice President Spiro T. Agnew.

[2] This image, to my mind, is preferable to that of the "melting pot," since we have seen that various ethnic and racial elements in America will not (happily, in my view) melt one into another, but will rather combine into a combination (like a stew) in which each preserves its own identity and flavors both the others and the general mixture. See chapter 4.

who wear doubleknits to the air-conditioned Mass on Sunday and drive home afterwards in big cars are Catholics. So are the people in the Orient whose Catholicism combines with the ancient tradition of ancestor worship.[3] So are the Indians whose Jesuit priests have adopted so many of the ways of the Hindu holy men.[4] So, too, are the Catholic Pentecostals and the Catholic Traditionalists.[5] Within Catholicism one may find theological and spiritual approaches which are distinctly Byzantine, Dominican, Roman, or transalpine.[6] So long as none of these approaches violates those precious few elements that are essential to being Catholic (that is, believing and acting as the whole Church always has in every place), the basic foundations can admit myriad superstructures and annexes. We have not the right to say that this or that approach or manifestation is not really Catholic, either because of its excessive conservatism (which many Catholic progressives have done) or for its lack of conformity to conservative stereotypes (as many Catholics, even in influential positions, have made the mistake of doing). The Catholics who follow the Jesuit swami may be repulsed by the American suburbanite parishioners and vice versa, but both groups are Catholic. We may argue that some people appreciate or apply the principles of Catholicism or Americanism to a much greater degree than some others do. This is a fact of life. But the zeal of some does not exclude from the ranks the common practices of others. Not all Americans are what we might call patriots; not all Catholics are what we might call saints.

It will be apparent from the foregoing, I believe, that when we are considering either Americanism or Catholicism, we have a certain tension in evidence between a dominant image (what most Americans or most Catholics seem to be or believe or do) and a somewhat self-conscious affirmation of difference from or protest against the dominant image (the sort of thing which, in terms of American culture in the late 1960s, was often called the "counter-culture").[7] Both sides, even with their excesses, can coexist, and by so doing can even generate a certain healthy tension which necessarily keeps a society (civil, religious, or otherwise) in the salutary business of self-examination and ongoing adaptation. The

---

3 See Mary Patricia Franz, "Religious Experience in Confucianism and Buddhism," in George Devine, ed., *New Dimensions in Religious Experience* (Staten Island, N.Y.: Alba House, 1971).

4 "The Jesuit Swamis of India," *Time*, April 23, 1973, p. 46.

5 For some description of each of these groups, see chapter 3.

6 A term used in Rome to describe the northern regions of Europe, e.g., France, Germany, Switzerland, the Netherlands, "across the Alps" (from Rome).

7 See Myron B. Bloy, Jr., "The Counter-Culture and Academic Reform," in *New Dimensions*, and Charles Reich, *The Greening of America* (New York: Random House, 1970).

problem comes, of course, when one of the parties says in effect to the other (to use the terms of transactional analysis), "I'm O.K.; you're *not* O.K.!" [8] This, it seems, is the kind of thing that happened between the police and the Yippies in Chicago in 1968 and that Robert E. Burns of *U.S. Catholic* has lamented as a tendency among Catholics to "read each other out of the Church." [9]

There is the somewhat understandable inclination, depending on one's standpoint, to fall into the trap of taking the side of one against the other, not just as a legitimate manner of preference, but in such wise as to question the other side's very right to exist, or into the other trap of uttering Mercutio's classic malediction, "A plague on both your houses!" [10] and simply going away. Our purpose here, though, is to look at some of the images, including dominant images and counterimages, and see what they might mean for American Catholicism in the future.

Again, while one should acknowledge the limitations of generalizations, it is helpful at once to distinguish between what I will call for our present purposes "coastal" and "heartland" social experiences. It is immediately apparent that I am distinguishing such regions as New York, San Francisco, and Boston from such regions as Denver, Kansas City, and Peoria; but the distinctions do not work with such simple and obvious facility. Los Angeles, on the Pacific Coast, is significantly more akin to the American "heartland" than is San Francisco, which lies four hundred miles to the north, largely because Los Angeles is to such a great extent a community of transplants from the Midwestern and Southwestern regions of the continent, whereas San Franciscans (like Bostonians) have often erected and cultivated a distinct civilization of their own unto the third, fourth, and even further generations. In the same way, Chicago probably resembles New York more than it resembles Peoria because its character as an urban center of economic opportunity has attracted pockets of ethnic and racial subcultures which would be found in coastal cities like New York.

In some societies within America (like Kansas City and Denver) there seems to be less reliance on the notions of the old country or the old neighborhood of residential stability, family interdependency, preservation of a previous cultural experience or expression, whether of the old country in Europe or of a previous American residence (as with

---

[8] Thomas A. Harris, *I'm Ok: You're Ok: A Practical Guide to Transactional Analysis* (New York and Evanston: Harper and Row, 1967).

[9] Robert E. Burns, "The Examined Life," *U.S. Catholic,* March, 1969.

[10] Mercutio, after having been fatally wounded in a skirmish between supporters of the rival houses of Montague and Capulet, curses them both. *Romeo and Juliet,* Act III, Scene 1.

members of the Dutch Reformed Church from Ada, Michigan, who take their sense of community with them to such colonies as the one in North Haledon, New Jersey),[11] and more reliance on the "American" canons of mobility, the nuclear family, and the sort of social and cultural homogeneity which becomes celebrated in pro football telecasts every Sunday and an occasional bucket of the Colonel's "finger-lickin' good" fried chicken. To identify some of these patterns of settling and living as characteristically American, however, is to take two dangerous steps: the first is to render a sociological and historical judgment, with what is still rather scant or tentative evidence; the second is to suggest that one form of life or social structure is more typically and thus more legitimately American than any other. In our previous observations we have hopefully warned against any such implication.

The dichotomy might be more clearly expressed in terms of one American experience and life pattern which is essentially stable in terms of a community, and usually in terms of a central city (e.g., the traditional notion of Boston as the "hub"), and another American experience which is essentially mobile, experimental, and not necessarily dependent on a central city. The city-centered pattern has been portrayed in the stage images of George Kelly's Philadelphia in his play *The Show-Off*,[12] wherein a family finds its residence, its stores, relatives, friends, and occupational and recreational opportunities all within a walk or public transit ride of one another, in an urban society (or more accurately a neighborhood within a city) which people would be loath to leave. The experimental life pattern has been explored in the film *Easy Rider* and others like it [13] in which individuals seek their objectives in ways which do not necessarily depend on a close-knit family, neighborhood, or community structure, and which almost always necessitate relocation, if not a chronic "roaming." These people have roots only in the broadest sense, in the nation or in a general geographical region, not in a state, city, or neighborhood. This style of American life is undeniably more prevalent today than it was even a decade or two ago, and has ramifications which may be at once invigorating (as noted in Padovano's *American Culture and the Quest for*

---

11 In 1966 I had the experience of visiting a community of members of the Dutch Reformed Church, whose American headquarters are in Ada, Mich., who had settled in North Haledon, not far from Paterson, New Jersey. They managed to an amazing degree to preserve their community as a transplant.

12 *The Show-Off* opened at the Playhouse Theatre in New York on February 4, 1924. It was published in paper by Samuel French, New York, 1925. Obviously, I am attending here to its sociological implications, rather than to the relationships between its characters. For a critical treatment of the play, see Arthur Wills, "The Kelly Play," *Modern Drama*, XVI: 3 (December, 1963).

13 *Easy Rider*, a 1969 Columbia film by Peter Fonda.

*Christid) [14] and dehumanizing (as pointed out in Packard's *A Nation of Strangers*).[15]

The life style one chooses, I believe, significantly influences the experience and expression of one's religion—including Catholicism—in America.

In a community-centered type of American life style, the individual envisions himself in terms of that specific community, which may be geographical, cultural, racial, ethnic, or socio-economic, as well as religious. This community, its structures and patterns, will always exert significant influence on the individual (although not necessarily vice versa), even if for some reason the individual should become physically separated from the community. An illustration of this would be the old saying, "You can take the boy out of Brooklyn, but you can't take Brooklyn out of the boy!"

In the more mobile type of American lifestyle, the family is described by sociologists and anthropologists as "nuclear," as opposed to "extended" (the father, mother, and children operate pretty much in isolation or independence, as opposed to a family which includes in its everyday operations grandparents, uncles, aunts, cousins, perhaps several neighbors, etc.). Relocation for reasons of education, occupation, or housing opportunity is both expected and frequent,[16] and close ties with communities or with personal individual friends are somewhat rare, since one knows that such ties are apt to be broken in the next move.[17]

In the more stable community it is possible and perhaps even desirable for the Church to play a key role in defining and being influenced by a variety of other aspects of community life—recreation, economics, politics, cultural and educational endeavors, and others. The Church is but one more stable aspect in a series of stable community patterns. Individuals or families with a mobile life style may *appear* to be more dependent on stability, at least externally, than those in close communities; in reality, however, they are more independent of social and cultural stability and more apt to expect and adapt to change. Moreover, the kind of stability they desire is likely to be of a much shorter-range variety than that which would be found in a community where one planned to spend a lifetime, and where one's parents (and perhaps grandparents) were born, raised, and buried. While the transient American many appear

---

[14] Anthony T. Padovano, *American Culture and the Quest for Christ* (New York: Sheed & Ward, 1969).

[15] Vance Packard, *A Nation of Strangers* (New York: McKay, 1972).

[16] Packard, ibid.

[17] Ibid. Also see the Harper's "wraparound" essay on "Friendship," *Harper's*, August, 1973.

to want the external signs of stability in his adopted community—before moving on to his next adopted community—he often wants them only in a superficial way, yet he remains open to change on deeper levels. In fact, one of the "stable values" in the transient's community is the very factor of mobility itself, so that even if he seems to be striving for stability, he is already predisposed to flexibility and experimentation (even if it is sometimes at his own peril). On the other hand, the inhabitant of a community whose stability is deep-rooted will find himself predisposed against flexibility and experimentation—except in superficial things like the sophistication of creature comforts—again at his own peril.

These observations lead us to distinguish two major styles of American religion (and in particular Catholicism), derived from two major styles of American life, which seem as though they will endure alongside each other at least in the immediate future, and perhaps even into the last decade of the present century. This distinction helps one to see the emergence of different patterns of Catholic thought and action concerning the matters which were discussed in the previous chapters of this book—the contemporary Catholic's attitudes toward the world in which he finds himself, relations between the individual Catholic and his Church as an institution in society, roles of the clergy, the religious-order members, and lay Catholics, and the attitudes and actions of the Church in liturgical and moral matters.

Needless to say, both respect for tradition and continuity, and receptivity to change and experimentation are essential elements for American Catholic life, and all life. There is no solace to be found in extolling the virtues of one life style while condemning the vices of the other. Moreover, it is significant that as our urban centers expand their spheres of influence, the sociological and psychological boundaries between one life style and the other tend to blur. In addition, as we have seen before, it will not be enough to talk in terms of "heartland" and "coastal" experiences and expressions of American Catholicism. However, these expressions are not used without foundation. By way of illustration, one might consider the contrast Thomas Fleming offers us in his sociological novel *The Sandbox Tree*.[18] Fleming's images are of a stultified, ossified city and its environs somewhere in the BosWash corridor [19] and the freedom and fresh air of the Rockies. As I have suggested before, the

---

[18] Thomas Fleming, *The Sandbox Tree* (New York: William Morrow and Company, 1970).

[19] BosWash corridor = the corridor of the northeastern U.S. which runs in a north-south line from Boston to Washington, taking in the metropolitan areas of Boston, Providence, New Haven-Bridgeport-Hartford, New York-New Jersey, Philadelphia, Wilmington, Baltimore, and Washington. The city in Fleming's novel is said to be an amalgam of elements from the various metropolitan areas just mentioned, intended to represent all of them but not to be limited in its identification to any one of them.

images are crude, oversimplified, and far too romantic. But there is something to the distinction. One sees it in the sort of "Chicago Catholicism" of which Andrew Greeley is an exponent; even though highly urbanized and even somewhat ghettoized, it is different from what one will find on either of America's seaboards. One begins to see it, too, even in crossing the Hudson from New York to New Jersey, or in crossing the bridge from San Francisco to the East Bay.

If I were to characterize the chief assets and liabilities of the two trends of Catholicism, I would suggest that where a Catholic subculture, especially an Irish-Catholic, Italian-Catholic, or Polish-Catholic subculture (or German-Catholic in some parts of the Great Lakes region) is still strong, there is a feeling of obligation to one's community, to one's ancestors, to one's (extended) family, and even to the very land itself. This feeling is seen at its best in the magnificent cathedrals in Newark and San Francisco, in the heroic acts of apostolic witness by clergy, religious-order members, and lay Catholics in cities like Oakland, Hoboken, and Milwaukee, and in serious commitments to Catholic education in urban centers like Jersey City. This feeling is seen at its worst when it manifests itself in excessive fear of newcomers to the immigrant pecking order, in too much concern for external continuity of Catholic life and not enough concern for the internal quality of that life, and in too much preservation of a Catholic pyramid of ascendancy with clearly defined obligations and opportunities for clergy, religious brothers and sisters, and lay Catholics.

Where Catholic subculture is not strong, however, as, for example, in what we have called the American "heartland," people rely less on distinctly Catholic neighborhoods, schools, colleges, hospitals, community organizations, recreational groups, newspapers and periodicals, and the like. One's obligations here are more to oneself and one's children than to one's ancestors and neighbors, and more to the places to which one may go in the future than to the place one resided in previously. This feeling is seen at its best in openness to ecumenism both in theory and in practice (including Catholics' openness to Jews and other non-Christians), receptivity to various forms of experimental ministry (for example, nonterritorial parishes and team ministries), or new patterns for the everyday life of the Church (lay religious educators, permanent deacons, pastoral councils, and greater activity by women in the Church). This feeling is seen at its worst in excessive anxiety for one's present and potential economic status, in too much concern for isolating one's children from the problems of a heterogeneous urban society and its hazards, and in the almost incredible gullibility of some in the face of anything which purports to be "new," "improved," "revised," or suggestive of progress (our most important product).

Anyone who has witnessed or experienced the life of the Catholic Church in places like Oklahoma, Indiana, Missouri, and Ohio, as contrasted with that in San Francisco, Boston, New York, and Philadelphia, can see the differences immediately. When these feelings, structures, and patterns mix, as in Chicago, New Jersey, or Los Angeles, the differences may be harder to trace, but they abide nonetheless.

American Catholics who have settled in, built, and intend to remain in and around the great urban centers of the country seem to feel (and not without cause) that their civilizations are eminently worth protecting, and these Catholics therefore admit only the sort of superficial change which is in accord with the changes the people themselves opt. In Brooklyn, for example, it was all right for the Vincentians to move a branch of St. John's University to Staten Island, because this is the type of place to which many Catholics in the region are themselves moving. But there is much ado over whether it "is still the same school," for example, whether or not it allows the boys to wear their hair long, or what the ratio is of "religious" to lay teachers. In Webster Grove, Missouri, the "secularization" of the college operated there by the Sisters of Loretto [20] stirred up much less apparent controversy than the "secularization" of Fordham University in New York sometime later.[21]

In light of such different attitudes toward these changes, and in light of the relative influence of the Catholic subculture in different communities, we must consider the potentialities of Catholics and Catholicism in America for change. One sees that the potentialities for change differ from region to region, subculture to subculture, and ultimately Catholic to Catholic. This leads to the thesis that change in the structures and patterns of American Catholic life will be much more rapid (and not always happily so) in the "heartland" than on either of America's coasts, and in the suburbs and rural areas than in America's urban centers. Put more simply, the Church in America will be more receptive to change the farther away it gets from the ocean. But, as we have seen with some urban exceptions to the rule (Los Angeles, hardly a typical coastal city, or Milwaukee, with substantial Polish-American

---

[20] See Garry Wills, *Bare Ruined Choirs: Doubt, Prophecy and Radical Religion* (Garden City, N.Y.: Doubleday & Co., Inc., 1972) for a description of the "secularization" of the College and the activity of its president, former Sister Jacqueline Grennan, S.L., now Jacqueline Grennan Wexler.

[21] In order to conform to New York State laws determining eligibility to receive State aid, Fordham University in 1968 became legally a "nonsectarian" private institution of education. This meant, practically, very little was changed. The transition appears to have been successful, despite some criticisms from both within and without that Fordham "sold out to the State" or "sacrificed its Catholic identity." In my opinion, the ends and means of Catholic higher education survive as well at Fordham as at most other Catholic colleges and universities in the United States.

and German-American communities), the formula cannot always be applied so simply.

Third-generation residents of the Parkchester district in the Bronx and fourth-generation residents of San Francisco (let alone fifth-generation residents of Boston!) are far more likely to send their children to parochial school than third-*year* residents of Danville (California) or Wheat Ridge (Colorado). Second-generation Chicago Catholics may send their children to a parish school, but they may also be more receptive to the idea of changing to public school eventually, and they are more likely to attend an ecumenical discussion group at their church. Residents of a new exurban parish may not bother to build a Catholic school at all. On the two seaboards there is apt to be more Catholic muscle-flexing on issues like pornography and abortion in the press and at the polls, and politicians will still seek a "Catholic vote." Ecumenism will likely be less official and more vital away from the coasts, where there will be less self-consciousness about who preaches from whose pulpit or who is a guest at what church. In Missouri, Nebraska, Arizona, and North Dakota, there already appear more opportunities for lay religious educators than in New York and California, despite the obvious disparity in population figures between the regions. The reason: clerical top-heaviness in the coastal centers of American Catholicism. This will almost certainly endure for some time, making the permanent deacon (particularly the married deacon) little more than an occasional window dressing in the Catholic communities of the Atlantic and Pacific shores of the country; but when one moves across the Hudson or across San Francisco Bay toward the middle of the country, he may be a real part of the Church's life.

The foregoing is not meant to imply that one region of Catholic America [22] is necessarily superior or inferior to another, more or less "advanced" theologically or spiritually, or more or less truly Catholic. It is meant to suggest, however, that American Catholicism will not move all together, all at once.

In light of the above, the following observations are offered as a tentative view of the future of American Catholicism in general, with special reference to the topics discussed in the previous chapters:

## 1. *American Catholics' outlook toward the world*

American Catholics, for the remainder of the twentieth century, will not be as likely as their predecessors to mistrust "the world"; nor will they be as likely as they were in the early 1960s to hope that the Christianiza-

---

[22] One may, but need not, associate this term with the uses and meanings given it by John Cogley in his book by that title, *Catholic America* (New York: Dial Press, 1973).

tion of the world, in a highly organized fashion and on a grand scale, would soon occur and thus unite man and his world in a sublime symphony of praise to the Creator. These two extreme outlooks having been rejected, it follows that certain extremes in practice will be rejected also. There will be less tendency to embrace groups or institutions or agencies which are distinctly Catholic for the sake of preserving Catholic interests which would otherwise not receive their fair share of protection. On the other hand, there will not be the extreme "secular city" tendency to ridicule or eschew Catholic organizations or services, opting instead for whatever the *saeculum* may have to offer.

For most Catholics, attitudes and actions will be determined in terms of their needs in concrete situations as they arise. In some communities, for example, the quality of public education may be so poor that Catholic parents who are sufficiently well-off may continue to make a substantial investment in parochial schooling. In other communities public schools may be so good that Catholic schools are no longer as essential as they once seemed, and a group of monied and concerned Catholic parents may even choose a broadened religious education program and let the parish school close.[23] The future of Catholic colleges, I suggest, will be similar, but a little more complex. Where a college is seen as protecting a distinct Catholic atmosphere for education, a community may well support it even at great sacrifice; in some other instances, the college may be operated by a combination of private donations and tuition monies plus federal and state funding, with the private funding from an individual, private concern for Catholic collegiate education and the public monies from general educational concerns (as I think will be the case in most of the Catholic colleges that stay in business).

Catholics in America will be in general less defensive than they were before the Council and less likely to run to the arms of Holy Mother Church whenever they feel the need for protection. They will be less likely to look up the NCOMP rating of a film in the diocesan newspaper; indeed, they will be less likely to *read* the diocesan newspaper, but those who do will read it more critically and had best be provided with more substantial Catholic journalism.

American Catholics will generally have less prejudices against both their neighbors and themselves in terms of what a Catholic in America may or may not, should or should not do and be. More and more, they will become Americans whose religious denomination happens to be Catholic, and not Catholics whose citizenship happens to be

---

[23] See John Deedy, "Catholic Schools: Down but not Out," *The New York Times,* August 12, 1973, for a good analysis and prognosis on Catholic schools.

American, not that there was ever a conflict between the two, but the terms of identification will be slightly different in their emphasis. The chief practical result of this will be the disintegration of all but a small core of Catholic political muscle on issues like abortion, pornography, aid to nonpublic schools, and similar questions (in an age when Catholics are already ceasing to "vote for their own kind" when a Catholic candidate runs against one who, in ages past, would have been identified only as a "non-Catholic").

The survival of institutions which represent "Catholic life in America" will be dependent on the goods they can deliver: Catholic hospitals will continue if they are excellent hospitals; Knights of Columbus councils may survive only on the strength of their air conditioning, the leanness of their sliced ham, and the flowing of their draft beer, and not on the awesomeness of the man who gives the fire-and-brimstone speech to the first-degree membership candidates. In general, many elements in social patterns which appear to be distinctively Catholic will be only marginally so, the evidences of a bygone era preserved for the sake of what they can offer to a larger number of people who for the most part will still be Catholics.

## 2. The roles of clergy, "religious," and laity in the Church

As suggested, American Catholics in general will cease to rely as heavily as they once did on the various institutions of their Church. Accordingly, the influence of clergy and religious brothers and sisters will become limited to more specific areas. The priest and—where he flourishes—the deacon will emerge primarily as leaders of community worship and motivators for individuals in the community to extend Christian charity and concern toward one another. Demands upon the clergy for spiritual leadership will be made by a generation of somewhat cynical lay American Catholics who feel that the rules of the game were changed on them at half time and that their clergy don't really know the new rules well either. However, there will be not a few opportunities for the clergy to be genuine spiritual, intellectual, and moral leaders when they are put to the test. Unfortunately, the tests may often be more demanding than what many of the clergy will be prepared for. This will mean that many clerics will find themselves utilized for the conducting of the liturgy, but that otherwise the laity will not have as much faith in them as they would have expected or preferred.

As previously suggested, there will likely be a surfeit of priests to take care of the needs of American Catholics, any "vocation shortage" notwithstanding. As Robert W. Hovda has observed, western Catholics engage in the strange practice of ordaining a man to the priestly ministry and then looking around to see if they can find a job for him, when Christian tradition seems to indicate that the reverse procedure makes more sense.[24] This means that, especially in the clerically top-heavy parts of Catholic America [25] described earlier in this chapter, there will be virtually no need for deacons or laymen to exercise some of the functions which are not essentially bound up with priesthood, although they might be able to exercise them quite well within the Catholic community. In other words, the nonpriest seeking to perform nonpriestly roles of leadership in the Church will usually have a chance to do so only when there are not enough priests to go around. Between the priests and the lay leaders in the Church there will be a sort of impasse: the priests will often feel that in operating the massive superstructure of Catholic educational institutions, they educated their own competition; the lay leaders will feel that in supporting the same superstructure of Church and schools, they financed *their* own competition (including the ex-priests who appear to get first crack at many nonpriestly positions in the Church). Although a few lay leaders will penetrate the barriers, most will be shut out by a sort of "benign neglect" and will go their own way. They quite possibly will continue to exert whatever influence they can on and for the Church, but in ways which do not place them at the mercy of the clergy (as in lay-operated enterprises like *The National Catholic Reporter,* rather than under any explicitly ecclesiastical auspices).

All of the above should indicate that there will be no real shortage of clergy in the American Church as a whole for the remainder of the century, and that there will therefore be no *pragmatic* reason (though there are theological reasons) to argue for the exercise of the priesthood by a broader base of candidates, for example, married men, or women. The permanent deacon, as we have seen, will hardly prove himself necessary in terms of his specifically sacramental functions, all of which can be performed just as well by a priest (note the twist which this puts on Pope Pius XI's principle of sudsidiarity!). However, the man or woman willing to be of special service to the community in doing the "dirty work"—inner city apostolates, working with the sick, aged, and retarded, working in religious education for little or no pay, organizing social action projects, serving the poor, running tutorial programs for the disadvantaged, operating drug abuse clinics—will always be in demand, lay or in vows, male or female, celibate or married.

[24] Robert W. Hovda, *Dry Bones* (Washington: The Liturgical Conference, 1973), chap. 1.

[25] See fn. 22.

These projections should make it clearer that the primary worth of the priest will be in leading the Christian community in meaningful worship and that the primary role of the religious man or woman— and that description will come to be understood far more broadly than in the recent past—will be in the witness of service to the needs of the community. The extent to which clergy and religious engender the support of the community for these roles will depend on how well the community sees their needs being fulfilled.

### 3.   *The liturgical lives of American Catholics*

The tendency of American Catholics neither to despise nor to embrace naïvely the *saeculum* will necessarily mean a heightened sense of need for truly meaningful and leavening liturgical experience. In some cases, the clergy will not be capable of providing this to the extent it is needed. In many more cases, the clergy will be capable of providing it if they themselves are given the chance. Part of the problem will be that the average American Catholic will not make known his need for a richer liturgical life because he himself will not be conscious of it. It will then be the responsibility of the clergy (and some lay leaders in the liturgy as well) to read the signals of this need and to respond accordingly. Some of the considerations which will probably emerge in this regard are:

A.   *An increased emphasis on flexibility in worship*   This means a certain flexibility in the styles and forms of worship, with a certain unity that will ensure that the central and essential elements of Catholic liturgical worship will always come through. It would be far too superficial to suggest that this will take the form of a "low-church, high-church, middle-or-broad church" division or of an "orthodox, conservative, reform" division; indeed, the purpose of liturgical diversity would be effectively defeated were the Church to divide into factions which each subsisted on a steady diet of only its own separate liturgical preference.

Again, without suggesting there need be division or factionalization of the Church, there will almost surely be more flexibility in terms of the exercise of the regular obligation to worship (a movement toward weekly, rather than Sunday or vigil observances) and one's membership in a worshipping community (a movement toward membership on grounds other than geographical location, for example, special interests, circles of friends and colleagues, etc.).

B.   *An increased emphasis on the role of the symbolic*   In a book

I edited entitled *Theology in Revolution*,[26] Andrew M. Greeley suggested that in the liturgical renovations of Vatican II, the Church managed to adapt itself to the secular spirit of the times just as man was about to get sick and tired of the secular spirit of the times. Furthermore, Greeley suggested, man found it necessary to supplant in his symbolic life the very things which the Church seemed to have removed prematurely: "... the hippies and the Merry Pranksters are putting on vestments and we're taking them off; we have stopped saying the Rosary and they're wearing beads ... we are making our new low-church liturgy as symbol-free as possible and they are creating their own liturgy which is filled with romantic poetry and symbolism." [27] The whole point, as mentioned in chapter three of this book, is that man needs symbols in his relationships with other men, and especially in relating to the divine. We have already seen a re-emphasis on the importance of the symbolic in Catholic worship over the past half-decade or so, and I believe we shall see more and more of it, although it will hardly be a simple repetition of the symbolism we have seen celebrated in the liturgy of the past. In all probability it will involve a happy combination of the more meaningful elements of traditional symbolism and the more potent symbols which are new and yet consonant with Christian liturgical tradition.

C. *Increased correspondence between liturgical celebration and various events of import in individual human lives* We commented in chapter two on the sacramental presence of the priest in "life's great moments," the Church's seven sacraments. In the future I believe this will not change significantly, but we will also see more liturgical or paraliturgical [28] celebrations pertaining to other moments in the life of an individual or a community. There will be ways of doing this which can be awfully maudlin, and we have doubtless seen some of that already; this sort of thing will surely fade away quickly. But I have in mind more meaningful liturgical celebrations or paraliturgical celebrations of the events of human and community life in light of the message and person of Jesus.

**4. *The posture of American Catholics on the ecumenical movement***

It is virtually impossible to approach this question without some

---

[26] George Devine, ed., *Theology in Revolution* (Staten Island, N.Y.: Alba House, 1970), pp. 26f; indem, *Transformation in Christ* (Staten Island, N.Y.: Alba House, 1972), pp. 21f.

[27] Devine, ed., *Theology in Revolution*, pp. 26f, and *Transformation in Christ*, pp. 21f.

[28] Paraliturgical means not a part of the official liturgy of the Church in itself, but somehow related or made to relate to it.

bias as to how much formal denominational uniformity is necessary among Christian religions before we can say there exists genuine and tangible ecumenical progress. My own bias is that formal denominational unity, desirable though it be, is not a prerequisite for some measure of genuine unity among Christian denominations in the United States. There is even considerable evidence to suggest that leading ecumenists today consider some unity between Christian denominations a *fait accompli,* and that they further consider formal denominational separation—to whatever extent it remains—more providential than problematic in some instances, for the sake of the smooth functioning of congregational bodies.[29]

Although we realize some obstacles to full ecumenical unity among Christians will still prevail, in any case for the foreseeable future, it is most important to remember the distinctions suggested in the earlier part of this chapter, namely, the variety of experiences and expressions which we tend to combine (legitimately!) under the generic heading of "American Catholicism." In this context, I suggest, true ecumenical unity is not something that has yet to happen by virtue of some ecclesiastical pronouncement, but neither is it fully accomplished. It is something which has begun to happen and will continue to happen at various rates of speed and with various manifestations of its progress in different situations.

There are already certain principles whereby the Roman Catholic Church will officially admit intercommunion.[30] Without arguing for loose interpretation of these permissions or anticipating future ones, it is not hard to see how the circumstances by which the Holy See will allow for intercommunion will soon come to be understood more broadly and applied more frequently than they are at the present time.

Our vision of ecumenism is narrow, however, if we do not see beyond the question of intercommunion or *communicatio in sacris,*[31] just as it would be narrow if we think only in terms of formal unity between denominational structures. The fact that numerous Protestant denominations (some quite kindred one to another), which do not have the same ecumenical problems that Roman Catholics have in "trying

---

[29] This was the general thinking reflected at the 1973 workshop of the Consultation on Church Union held at Seton Hall University, and later that year at the COCU plenary session in Memphis.

[30] See Sara Butler, "Intercommunion in an American Perspective," in George Devine, ed., *That They May Live: Theological Reflections on the Quality of Life* (Staten Island, N.Y.: Alba House, 1972), pp. 235–44.

[31] Literally sharing or communing in sacred things, e.g., the sacraments, especially the Holy Eucharist or Holy Communion in the Mass-liturgy. For a good discussion of this classic theological notion in broad contemporary terms, see Raimundo Panikkar, *Worship and Secular Man* (Maryknoll, N.Y.: Orbis Books, 1973).

to get together with Protestants," have not achieved formal interdenominational unity among themselves does not mean that they have not achieved ecumenical progress in a most genuine sense. This also illustrates, I think, that there can be, and often is, real ecumenical unity between Christian communities of different denominations, particularly on the local or grass-roots level, in ways which are quite different from formal denominational or structural unity. This means a clear understanding of the legitimacy of a fellow Christian's different approach to the person and gospel of Jesus, and the willingness to draw strength from a different Christian witness in addition to one's own so that both may be enhanced. By extension, the same principle may apply to relations between Christian and non-Christian believers, for example, between Christians and Jews. This kind of thing may or may not manifest itself in such activities as joint inner city or community projects, but it surely must always go beyond "nice" unity octave celebrations. This kind of ecumenism is already present in large measure and happily growing for many American communities in which Catholics have a share. In many other communities with a substantial Catholic population, there is still too much smugness and suspicion for this sort of healthy ecumenical atmosphere to develop, or even worse, there sometimes is a presumption that all that is needed has been done and no more is necessary. It will be necessary for Catholics (and others) in America to move forward in this regard while realizing that one's own movement forward cannot have its pace retarded by the slowest members of the contingent.

### 5.  *The moral consciousness of American Catholics*

As we have observed in the chapter immediately preceding, the moral consciousness of American Catholics, until the mid-1960s, was extremely rigid and "cut and dried." That it is no longer so is a matter of record. I would suggest, however, that the Church in America is in danger of losing whatever moral force it might have by concentrating its moral guidance too much and in too negative a way on issues pertaining to man's use of his generative faculties and not enough on moral issues in the broader sense. In other words, we are in danger of having a Church whose moral sense is arrested at the genital stage.[32] At this writing, the Church seems to have allowed her members to make up their own minds on a variety of important moral issues without its own guidance, not because the Church prized individual freedom

---

[32] See my remarks in the article, "On Abortion—Church Authorities Must Do Much More," *The National Catholic Reporter,* April 20, 1973, and in the letter "Liberate All Priests, Not Only Some," ibid., August 4, 1972.

of conscience, but simply by default on the part of the institutional Church. This has been manifest, I believe, in the characteristic reluctance of Catholic churchmen to discuss some social issues for fear of not seeming to be united in their position. The result has been a sort of void in moral leadership. At the same time, too much emphasis on issues like contraception and abortion, on what man might do *wrong* with his generative faculties and not enough positive emphasis on what he might do *right,* has made too many people feel that the Church simply has no place talking about the moral significance of the private actions of the individual, and that the Gospel may have no wisdom to offer that may be applied to individual lives. Ironically, the Church has done such a job of "overkill" in terms of sexual morality that hardly anyone listens anymore. There was a certain strength in a Catholic system of morality which envisioned justice as guided by principles of natural moral law,[33] and which attempted to guard against the devaluation of sexual symbols in interpersonal encounter. Unfortunately, these strengths are seldom in evidence today, and what remains in their place seems little more than a painful awareness of the fragility and myopia of a morality which attempted to teach too much too harshly with too much attention to one area of human activity.

Whether they or their Church like it or not, many American Catholics will become increasingly selective in listening to and acting on whatever moral pronouncements come from their often confused and confusing leaders. The best that the Church in America might hope for in the remainder of this century, in my view, would be an affirmation of the principles of justice for all men, which would help alleviate some of the human strife which the Church should address and not ignore. However, I doubt whether this will succeed. And if it does not, the Church is not likely to be listened to on very much else.

Having made these observations in light of our previous areas of concern, we might now explore some further ramifications of the American Catholic experience as it appears to be shaping up for the rest of the twentieth century.

1.  What is the future of the relationship of American Catholic life to that of the rest of the world Catholic Church, or, simply put, what is—and will remain to be—distinctively American about American Catholicism?

2.  How do the religious and social trends among Catholics in America compare with those among other religious groups in

---

[33] See Devine, ed., *That They May Live,* chaps. 6 and 7.

America, and to what degree are these tendencies, when shared, characteristic of American culture and society as a whole?

3.  What do the answers to the above questions portend for Catholicism and for America?

## 1.  *The distinctive contributions of American Catholicism*

It has been remarked by some observers that Americans were not among the intellectual leaders at the Second Vatican Council, or in the liturgical renewal movement, or in the biblical renaissance of the late nineteenth and the earlier twentieth centuries. It has also been lamented of late that American Catholic religious leadership has often been more docile than its counterparts in many other countries. Withal, American Catholicism enjoys a special vigor which is directly a result of the total American experience and also of the separation of the American Catholic Church from both the central authority of the Church in Rome and the more docile countries across the Atlantic which are the parents of American Catholicism (specifically Ireland). Needless to say, this will be especially evident in regions which are less conscious of constant Roman domination and inclined to be more independent in the local translation of Roman authority, although the Church in these regions will remain respectful of the necessary dimensions of central authority in the Church Catholic. This kind of particularly American spirit within Catholicism will be more in evidence in the "heartland" type of Catholicism than in the coastal type which is more Roman- and Irish-dominated. This spirit has been slow in growing and may continue to be slow even in more progressive areas, but it is there. It showed itself earlier in this century in the origination of such movements as the YCS, YCW, YCM (Young Christian Students, Young Christian Workers, and Young Christian Movement) and the Catholic Interracial Council, Friendship House, Vernacular Society, and kindred groupings in and around Chicago. It will continue to show itself in the witness of individual bishops like Thomas Gumbleton and Carroll Dozier in their concern for social justice, priests like Robert Fox and John Egan in their work for the disadvantaged, and such phenomena as nonterritorial parishes [34] and democratically oriented parochial and diocesan councils and synods.

American Catholicism, where it is more American than trans-

---

[34] See the reports on the status of nongeographical parishes in the United States compiled and commented on by *The National Catholic Reporter,* October 26, 1973, and also my own remarks in *Liturgical Renewal: An Agonizing Reappraisal* (Staten Island, N.Y.: Alba House, 1973).

planted-European, will bring to America and to Catholicism a spirit which is experimental, mobile, and democratic. At the same time, the European and traditional elements of Catholicism will be able to bring to American Catholicism and to America a concern for history and a reluctance to discard the baby with the proverbial bath-water.

American Catholicism, if it does not consider itself inferior to or a weak carbon copy of European Catholicism, will be bold in its experimentation—sometimes too bold—but the excess will be easier to correct than any insufficiency would be. If American Catholicism does not measure itself against the Holy Roman Empire or the European Church of the Counter-Reformation, it will be at least as open to ecumenism as the Catholicism of any of the seemingly more advanced countries in the world. And throughout all of this, American Catholicism will enjoy and must take advantage of a heritage steeped in a great tradition which will be an essential ingredient for the future of all American life and American Catholic life in particular.

## 2. *American Catholicism and other religious groups in America*

It must be admitted that American Catholics are in a sense not really charter members of the American enterprise. It was largely a group of Protestants from England, after all, who began the colonization and revolted for the independence of the land two centuries ago. This is not to suggest that there were no Catholics on hand at the outset: indeed, history tells us otherwise. However, the dominant thrust of the original American effort and experience was Protestant; American Catholics frequently felt they had to remind their Protestant compatriots that the articles of the Constitution apply to all who have come here seeking life, liberty, and the pursuit of happiness with full freedom of religious belief and practice.

These factors have brought some curious results, not the least of which has been the fact that the early fears of papism on American soil often generated, until at least the recent past, what they hoped to avoid. Ostracized or relegated to second-class citizenship in a Protestant-dominated America which professed religious liberty for all, American Catholics found themselves invited, if not virtually forced, by their Protestant compatriots to look across the Atlantic to the old country or to the Holy See at Rome when they sought to understand their own identity. A greater realization of Catholic participation in the American enterprise from the outset would likely have reduced this tendency, but instead, religious bigotries and tensions were allowed to develop as all too real ingredients in the history of America as we have come to know it.

It is precisely this history which accounts in large measure for the distinction which I and others (Greeley, Padberg, Lawler, et al.,[35] each in his own different way and from his own special perspective) have seen and reported between "coastal" and "heartland" Catholicism, or between a type of Catholicism which feels very much at home in the common American experience and the type which cannot feel at home in it without some measure of ethnic or national identity. Thus there will be a tendency among Catholics in coastal and urban areas of America to be at least as rigid as (and probably a good deal more rigid than) members of other religious groups in the same areas. In most of the heartland, Protestants and Catholics, and Jews too, will probably be more receptive to change, including the sort of change which brings them together in various cooperative or ecumenical ventures to whatever extent these are theologically and practically possible. As observed, there may be pockets of rigidity even in the vast expanses of Mid-America, just as there may be flexible communities on the coasts. These will serve, for various reasons, as exceptions to the rule: Chicago because it is both Midwestern and a port city, like New York and San Francisco; Los Angeles because it is a city on a coast of transplants from noncoastal areas, and so forth. In general, however, American religions will often share the tension between rigidity and flexibility evident among Catholics in the United States, for both are necessary elements in their development. The chief difference will be that these tendencies, while flourishing among the conditions afforded by different environments, will have come to be what they are, when and where they are, by different routes through history. One important factor to remember here is that Protestants, feeling essentially at home anywhere and at any time in America, will tend to be less rigid than Catholics, although there may exist tensions between different Protestant denominations in particular areas. Another is that Catholics, once having moved from the "old country," may be slightly less comfortable than Protestants with the national tendencies toward mobility. More Protestants than Catholics followed their apparent manifest destiny from sea to shining sea, and Protestants more often feel that one part of the country is just about as much home as another. Although various processes of social assimilation and socio-economic upward mobility indicate increased geographical mobility among Catholics, there still would appear to be less inclination among Catholics to pack up and move within America. That this will have implications for various factors relating to Catholics' lives in America (social, commercial, even intellectual) should not be difficult to envision.

---

[35] See chapter 4 in this book.

These tendencies of rigidity among American Catholics—tendencies which lend themselves more to empathy than to empirical analysis—may well result in a certain intransigence among the Catholic "ethnics" of many parts of America, especially on the coasts and in the cities, if they are not sufficiently challenged or properly directed. Like fire or nuclear energy, this intransigence can be a valuable natural resource for us if it is properly understood and utilized. It may well be that a certain emphasis among Catholics in America on tradition, history, continuity, beauty versus utility, or individualism versus utilitarianism will prove a most necessary leaven for the intellectual and spiritual lives of Americans for a long time to come. As trends of religious and moral thought and action develop, American Catholics to some extent may appear to be—and may in fact be—stubbornly out of step with the rest of Americans; at the same time, they can perform an essential function of critical conscience for American religion in general. The kind of religious witness we have seen of late concerning the value of the individual human life in such moral issues as war, abortion, civil rights, the right to alternative nonpublic education, euthanasia, urban planning and relocation, and numerous related questions, is hardly an exclusively Catholic prerogative. The Catholic contribution to the thinking out of these matters has been too much limited to certain topics, and cannot in any case be expected to always have its way in a free and pluralistic society; but without that Catholic contribution alongside others, American moral consciousness and our appreciation of the individual in light of spiritual and ethical values could not be what it is.

### 3. The future for Catholicism and for America

Whatever the strengths and shortcomings of America and of Catholicism have been in the past and may be today, it is at least clear that the two need not be parties to an adversary relationship, as they so often appeared to be in ages past. It will be argued that a certain type of Catholic-oriented pressure still exists in the United States, even if it is less significant or powerful than it was in the 1950s, for example. In certain areas, it will be noted, Catholics manage to enjoy thinly-veiled State or municipal aid for their schools (although it must be done so as to benefit all nonpublic schools, avoiding any obvious constitutional problems). In particular localities, Catholics manage to elect someone who appears to be a good Catholic candidate or to favor Catholic interests; conversely, election may be effectively denied someone who appears unsympathetic to Catholics or their interests. On a national scope, Catholics appear militant in attempting to make the legal case against the permission of abortion and in bringing pressure to bear on those who seem to advance the other side of this sort of moral question (witness the flap over CBS-TV rebroadcasting two episodes dealing with abortion in their *Maude* series in 1973). But is it not clear that such evidence is more newsworthy today than it was in the past simply because it is less common? And is it not clear, also, that its effect is far less widespread than it would have been two decades ago?

Despite the occasional examples of Catholic retrenchment which have surfaced during the early 1970s, and which will doubtless show themselves in the future from time to time, the days of a Catholic bloc moving in lock step are gone for good in America, and in most other places as well. This diversity will necessarily bring an end, over and above the termination of many ideological differences, to many adversary relationships that may have been apparent between Catholicism as a force and America as a political system or national experience.

What happens in various demonstrations of apparent Catholic retrenchment is, more often than not, something quite different from what it would seem to be. The attempt to support distinctively *Catholic* schools is often an attempt to support private schools that happen to be under Catholic auspices. The campaigns for or against candidates are often based on their complete socio-economic or ethnic profiles, of which Catholic religious affiliation seems to be only one easily identifiable element. The questions of abortion (or pornography, or whatever) are often anything but specifically Catholic questions, although it must be admitted that Catholic churchmen will often utilize their roles in the community to advance their viewpoint, just as some of them will utilize the issues themselves as ways of unifying the charges • under their ecclesiastical leadership. It is not possible, however, for a Catholic prelate or politician to move the whole of Catholic America to any particular end—if, indeed, this were *ever* really possible or even desirable! American Catholics today are about as predictable as American Jews, American Methodists, American members of the Church of Jesus Christ of Latter-Day Saints (Mormons), or Americans who happen to have converted from Christianity to Islam, when it comes to speaking of large blocs. We must, instead, speak of *individuals* (or small collections of individuals, in particular regions or neighborhoods) who are Catholic or who are exponents of different Catholic contributions and influences (some edifying, some inhibiting, some a mixture of the two).

When speaking of America and Catholicism in America, we will necessarily speak in terms of a balance of influences. America has already been influenced in no small measure by the faith, folkways, priorities, and practices of Americans who have been Catholic. This influence, for better *and* for worse, will doubtless continue, as both an individual and a collective influence giving to Americans at large both everything that is sublime about the ideology and ideals of Catholic Christianity and everything that is ridiculous about the feeble attempts of human members of the Church to carry out those ideologies and ideals. At the same time, Catholicism has been influenced in faith and practice (even when only by way of reaction) by the themes of freedom, exploration, democracy, mobility, and pragmatism which have emerged as characteristically American. This influence, too, is mixed, bringing with it the thrill that comes from the recollection of 1776, Abraham Lincoln, or the Alliance for Progress, as well as the nausea that comes from the recollection of a too long tolerated series of racial and religious bigotries, or the moral depravity characterized by such historical blemishes as Watergate. In the balance, even when the negative influences that flow in both directions have been fully measured, the nature of Catholicism and the nature of America both indicate that America and Catholicism are already richer for their having grown together and can be of great benefit to each other for the growth that both must know in the future.